THE INDUSTRIAL ARCHITECTURE OF YORKSHIRE

John Smith's Brewery, Tadcaster.

The Industrial Architecture of Yorkshire

Jane Hatcher

Phillimore

1985

Published by
PHILLIMORE & CO. LTD.
Shopwyke Hall, Chichester, Sussex

ISBN 0 85033 527 2

*Publication of this book has been
made possible through the generous
support of:*

JOHN SMITH'S
TADCASTER BREWERY LIMITED
THE BREWERY
TADCASTER
NORTH YORKSHIRE LS24 9SA
TELEPHONE:
TADCASTER (0937) 832091
TELEX: 55349

Printed and bound in Great Britain by
THE CAMELOT PRESS LTD.
Southampton, England

CONTENTS

LIST OF ILLUSTRATIONS

frontispiece: John Smith's Brewery, Tadcaster

BACKGROUND

SOURCES OF POWER

MISCELLANEOUS INDUSTRIES

INTRODUCTION

The material in this volume is a selection from that accumulated during a two-year research appointment with the Yorkshire Arts Association beginning in 1972. The Visual Arts Panel of the Association had become acutely aware of the increasing rate of destruction of the country's industrial heritage, then being carried out in an attempt to remove so-called eyesores, and to eliminate what was regarded as a stigma—the northern image of. dark satanic mills. The aim of the project was to record as many as possible of the buildings likely to disappear.

The rate of destruction slowed somewhat as the country's economic prosperity declined, but still the clearance continued, sometimes for road schemes, occasionally for new industrial units, often for housing developments on cheap land. Nationalised industries were under particular pressure to tidy away derelict property. Many buildings included in this book will have been demolished since the research was done, but that was what the project was all about. In a few cases buildings have been restored and converted to new uses.

The selection of material is imperfect; there are omissions of historically important sites, and inclusions of little-known buildings. The author acknowledges subjectivity, and apologises to those readers who will be saddened or annoyed at the discovery that their particular favourite is missing! Some industries are omitted if they have left behind few buildings of little architectural interest.

As a preliminary to the project to record Yorkshire's industrial architecture, the Yorkshire Arts Association commissioned Margaret Gathercole to produce a travelling exhibition of photographs on the same theme: I am grateful to her for permission to use several of her superb illustrations.

The research project was initiated by Michael Dawson, then Director of the Yorkshire Arts Association, and was supervised by Dr Patrick Nuttgens, Director of Leeds Polytechnic, who contributed a great deal of help and encouragement. In addition, I would like to express my gratitude to my sponsors: the original research was substantially funded by Bass Charrington (North) Ltd., and this publication has received generous support from John Smith's Tadcaster Brewery and West Yorkshire County Council.

To acknowledge my debt to all those who helped with the project would greatly increase the length of the text. Instead, the book is dedicated to the many people who contributed information, told me of interesting buildings, or showed me round buildings in their charge.

JANE HATCHER

I

BACKGROUND

THAT ENORMOUS SOCIAL and economic upheaval, generally called the Industrial Revolution—the phenomenon which produced most of the buildings in this book—took place over several generations, in some industries before others, and in some places before others. Before it occurred, most industrial processes were carried out on a small scale, in insignificant buildings, using small tools powered by hand. After it had happened, the majority of industries were located in centres specialising in a particular product, and were housed in large buildings powered by steam engines. In general, the Industrial Revolution resulted in industries moving to new areas, into large new buildings dedicated to a specialist process, achieved by machines.

The historical sequence of events is largely a series of chicken-and-egg situations. Improved machines required better motive power; better motive power enabled machines to be improved. Improved means of motive power encouraged the relocation of industrial buildings to sites better disposed to either water or steam power. Sites with good water power facilities tended to be remote and required improved access; improved communications were also needed to transport coal for steam power. Better access also enabled bigger quantities both of raw materials to be brought in and of finished products to be taken out.

Improvements in motive power caused larger industrial buildings to be constructed, and the new locations provided an incentive to experiment with new building forms and materials. In addition the canals, and later the railways, generated their own new types of architecture.

In architectural terms, then, the overall effect of the industrial revolution was a transition from domestic-scale buildings to large factories, but there were also fundamental economic and social changes. Cottage industries do not require fixed hours of working, and people had generally worked in small groups, productivity varying with demand, and with alternative needs—such as those of the harvest for every spare pair of hands. Working long hours inside a factory resulted in a very different lifestyle, although more actual cash might be earned that way.

Everyone knows about the ill-effects suffered by the factory hands in their new type of employment, but the originators of the change are more obscure, except for a few famous names. There must have been hundreds of unknown individuals who made slow, slight changes which contributed to the overall pattern of upheaval. The medieval guild system in the towns and cities still had considerable influence well into the 17th and 18th centuries. Craftsmen took apprentices, whom they often continued to employ as journeymen after they had been trained over a period of several years. The emphasis was on conservative continuity, not on innovation.

1

In country districts, craftsmen were mainly employed by the manorial estates, and only with reluctance were outside skills brought in for expensive specialist tasks. In villages people derived much of their livelihood from the land, growing produce for their own needs, and bartering it amongst their neighbours, people their families had known for generations, and with whom they were most likely intermarried. It is somewhat ironic that it was in country districts where people might, in the right circumstances, be more responsive to the stimulus of new ideas than in the towns, where the population was more transient. In towns there was also more of a temptation to accumulate property, and to serve on local government and poor-law bodies. In the country this was left to the local squire, who might sometimes seek to dabble in a new venture, or to try out an idea he had read about, and his workers did what they were told. On country estates the people were also more used to working in considerable numbers for a single owner, a system which perhaps provided the foundation for the factory system more often than has been recognised. In the rural areas also were the wind- and water-powered sites which had mostly been used for grinding corn into flour. Here, too, might be the folk memories of industrial activity on Cistercian monastic sites, and in the country there could occasionally be moments of slack demand, when there was the opportunity to experiment.

In the towns market demands were more constant, so people worked more steadily, and were less affected by seasonal variations. However, in the towns there was another category of innovation—members of the capitalistic middle class, many of whom had acquired property and status in Tudor and Stuart times. The corn mill had long been a valued commodity, which enjoyed a manorial monopoly, and one which could be expanded to absorb growing demand from the increasing population of nearby towns. Many suitably-placed Yorkshire corn mills were greatly enlarged in the 17th century, an example being Ulshaw Mill in Wensleydale, which had served a depopulated village near Ulshaw Bridge. In 1648 the mill was acquired by Francis Watson of the nearby town of Middleham, an entrepreneur who preferred to describe himself as a gentleman. Surviving records show that about 1655 he rebuilt the mill to three times its original capacity, to supply flour to Middleham, which had an inadequate manorial mill. Watson must have been delighted when, in 1674, the old timber bridge was rebuilt, as the new stone bridge greatly improved access between the mill on one bank of the River Ure, and Middleham on the other. The ruinous remains of Ulshaw Mill survive today, and show that it bore a remarkable similarity to a mill illustrated in a German book of corn mills published in 1617. However, the technology used had changed but little from medieval times: what is significant is the increase in the scale of operation.

In Yorkshire, the textile industry illustrates very clearly the change from domestic to factory system. There were distinct advantages in housing employees in a special building and supervising their work. This ensured that they produced goods to the necessary standard, and worked the hours required, which was particularly important if the employer was laying out the capital to buy expensive machines, and even more so if he were paying for the development of improved machinery.

A few factories were built before the development of powered machines, when hand-power was still dominant. At Lumb, near Huddersfield, there is an early 'manufactory', built next to the clothier's farmstead, in which weavers produced

2

1. Ulshaw Bridge over the River Ure.

2. This pedestal, in one of the cutwaters on Ulshaw Bridge, bears the inscription *RW 1674*, which commemorates the building of the present stone bridge, which replaced a medieval timber structure.

cloth on handlooms, but in his premises instead of within their cottages. The architecture is not obviously 'industrial', but is clearly derived from the local vernacular design of cottages in which the upper storey contains 'weaving' windows.

An early textile mill building survives at Gayle, near Hawes in Wensleydale. Built as a cotton mill in 1785, it derived its power from the small stream running through the village. When little water was coming down it, the flow could be diverted by the unusual means of a narrow cleft gouged out of the rock forming the stream bed, into an artificial dam, where it could accumulate. The water could then be released back when needed into the stream, and taken down the head race to the mill, which still uses water to power a turbine driving massive saws, for the mill is now used as a joiner's workshop.

Gayle Mill is larger in scale that most domestic buildings, but in architectural terms it is clearly based on typical 18th-century lines—a fairly narrow plan with regularly-spaced 'Georgian' windows in the front and back walls, providing daylight throughout the building. Thus the new industrial building type borrows from the domestic.

3. German corn watermill from a book published in 1617.

4. Ruins of Ulshaw Mill.

5. Ulshaw Mill: arches through which the tail race left the mill. The masonry survives from *c.* 1655, and when built the mill must have looked very like the German mill illustrated here.

6.   Lumb, near Huddersfield: an early manufactory, in which cloth was woven on handlooms in the late 18th century, under the supervision of the clothier, whose farmstead is next door.

7.   Gayle, near Hawes: an early water-powered textile mill built in 1785. Note the regularly-spaced windows, of Georgian proportions, which light the interior from both the front and back. The overshot waterwheel was formerly in the end of the building nearest the stream, and water was taken to it by an elevated leat from a point above the waterfall in the background.

8. The Duerley Beck near Gayle: a narrow cleft, gouged out of the rock forming the stream bed, directs water into a channel (in the foreground) leading to an artificial pond.

9. The pond, with the village of Gayle behind: when the stream is low, water from the pond can be emptied back into the stream, and taken off to the leat in the usual way.

When Gayle Mill was built, cotton was the most mechanised type of textile produced, though it must have been very laborious transporting cotton by pack-horse to upper Wensleydale. The mill soon went over to woollen yarn as that technology caught up, and supplied knitters in the stocking trade. Stocking manufacture was a strong tradition in the upper dales, which supplemented subsistence agriculture and mineral extraction. However, in 1785 few of the processes involved even in the production of cotton cloth could be achieved on powered machines, and it seems likely that only some of the preparatory stages would be water-powered, and the spinning still done on hand-powered machines. Later, perhaps, the wool was spun there by water power.

In Hawes itself there are two other buildings which were early textile mills. Nevertheless, upper Wensleydale was too remote to continue as a textile centre as other areas gained first canal, and later railway, communications. Larger mills were built in those areas with good transport facilities, and they flourished, able to obtain cheap coal for steam engines to manufacture on a larger scale than their water-powered rivals.

Another form of transition from a domestic scale of operation to the factory system is illustrated in the Abbeydale complex at Sheffield, where a number of small workshops were grouped together into a larger complex. A waterwheel provided power for tilt-hammers, but steel was produced 'by hand' in small crucibles, and sharp-edged tools such as scythes and sickles were manufactured in small blacksmith's shops—for use by hand on the land.

Most industries experienced a period of diversification in the late 18th century, with an increase in the number of industrial units, many of which were in themselves no larger in scale than their forebears. Later, the few units with optimum conditions prospered and expanded, while many of the other small units closed down. Sometimes this was as much due to the personal qualities of individuals as to general conditions. In the late 19th century, even industries like brewing, which had previously been practised in every settlement, generally contracted to specialist centres such as Tadcaster. Even the once ubiquitous village corn mill closed down, as people were able to buy mass-produced flour more cheaply from large mills with easy access to good communications; for example, those at Hull.

10. Hawes: early textile mill.

11. Hawes: early textile mill later used for the revival of the manufacture of Wensleydale cheese in the early 20th century — the name WENSLEYDALE DAIRY can still be seen on the building.

12. Abbeydale Industrial Hamlet, Sheffield: the building with steps in front of it contains the crucibles which were heated from below by furnaces served by the elongated chimney stack. Outside is a trough of water, used for soaking the sacking which the men wrapped around their legs before lifting the heated crucibles out of the furnaces. (*Sheffield City Libraries*)

13. Abbeydale Industrial Hamlet, Sheffield: early 19th-century Bill Head with engraving showing the dam for the waterwheel on the left with the crucible room in the centre. On the right a small building with several small forges within it can be seen. *(Sheffield City Libraries)*

II

SOURCES OF POWER

General Introduction

THE DISCOVERY of sources of power in addition to those of humans—and animals—was instrumental in the evolution of industrialised society. Civilisations other than those of Northern Europe were responsible for developing means of harnessing naturally-occurring potential power, freely available from water and wind. All we can claim in Yorkshire is that we made full use of such innovations.

The concept of water power was the first of these to be introduced to the county, by the Romans. Water power reigned supreme for nearly 1,000 years, until in the 12th century it was joined by wind power. Water and wind were freely, if irregularly, available as sources of power. They did their job efficiently, and left no pollution behind. Both were used primarily for the most basic need, that of grinding corn in order to make bread. From the 13th century water power was used in the textile industry; for five centuries solely to drive fulling stocks, the only existing machines suitable for mechanical manipulation. As machines were developed, the waterwheel played an increasing part. Bellows for furnaces and tilt hammers in forges made use of water power from the late Middle Ages; it was also used to facilitate drainage in mine-shafts. Wind power, too, was adapted to a greater range of uses, particularly for field drainage as agriculture became more efficient.

Wind and water power are almost entirely mutually exclusive. Water power is available where there are streams and rivers falling from higher to lower ground, such as the Yorkshire Dales and North York Moors. Where such water is not available, as on the flat tops of the Wolds or in the Vale of York, conditions are suitable for wind power, a phenomenon borne out by the gaunt, eye-catching towers of old windmills dotted around these areas.

Steam engines were originally used to assist drainage in mines, and later improved to the extent that they were reliable enough to power factories. West Yorkshire's survival as a textile centre was due very largely to its being well-placed for the adoption, of steam power, with local coal supplies, and iron-ore deposits necessary to construct the iron horse.

Wind, water and steam are all obsolete as major power sources in Yorkshire today. Only one windmill retains its sails, and that in a museum rather than a commercial context. A handful of waterwheels are workable. A few steam engines are still at work, but most have been scrapped, many the victims of Clean Air legislation. All three in their day prompted the design of new forms of architecture: the windmill tower above which the sails could rotate, the mill building which could straddle a water course, the engine house to accommodate a volatile machine separated from the rest of the building for reasons of safety. Wheel, sails and engine have all been accorded respect

12

by the workers who depended on them, and this was reflected in the architecture provided for the prime movers; architecture now obsolete and frequently abandoned.

The production of town gas made little impact on the geographical distribution of industry, unlike its predecessors in power history. It was not used to any great extent to power a prime mover, being more suitable for artificial lighting. Its contributions were the economic and social changes resulting from flexible working hours which industry experienced for the first time after having been reliant solely on daylight. The claim of gas to a place in the annals of industrial history is a rather special one: the buildings associated with its production have been destroyed more rapidly than any other species of industrial architecture. With the advent of North Sea gas, town gas works went out of use in the space of less than a decade, and have nearly all been destroyed. Often a lone gas-holder is all that remains, and many of these, too, have been removed.

Finally, into the history of power architecture came electricity. Around the turn of the present century each town and city added a power station to its gas works. There were links with older sources of power, for electricity was at first produced from coal by steam engines and from water by turbines. It was a much more versatile power source than anything which had preceded it, providing light and heat as well as motive power. However, 20th-century technology has now also overtaken municipal power stations, and they, too, are being taken out of use in favour of more economical generating complexes which feed the National Grid.

Water

The availability of supplies of water suitable for powering waterwheels in the Pennine tributary valleys was a major factor in the rise of revolutionised industry in Yorkshire. Water power was introduced into Yorkshire by the Romans. They absorbed the cultures of civilisations they had conquered, and spread their spheres of influence. The Romans had not invented the waterwheel, but they were responsible for its widespread use for grinding corn, in quarrying and mining, and for pumping water from lower levels up into aqueducts, in far corners of their empire. Despite the density of Roman occupation in this county, no water-powered sites have as yet been positively identified here. The nearest Roman corn-mill is on Hadrian's Wall, and there was a pump-supplied aqueduct at Lincoln.

At Wharram Percy on the Yorkshire Wolds, a deserted medieval village site is being excavated year by year by Leeds University. Excavation has so far proved that the site was occupied at least from the 6th century A.D. and a Saxon watermill site complete with grain has been found, although so little remains that it is difficult to interpret. All around Wharram Percy are the sites of Roman villas and farmsteads, and cultivation terraces can clearly be seen, indicating that the area was intensively farmed as arable land. It is just possible that eventually the site will yield the remains of a Roman water-powered corn mill!

By the time of the Domesday Survey of 1086, there were about 100 mills in Yorkshire. They must have been water-powered, as the windmill did not arrive until the 12th century, and they had presumably been established before the Norman Conquest. The spread of knowledge of the waterwheel must therefore be seen as

13

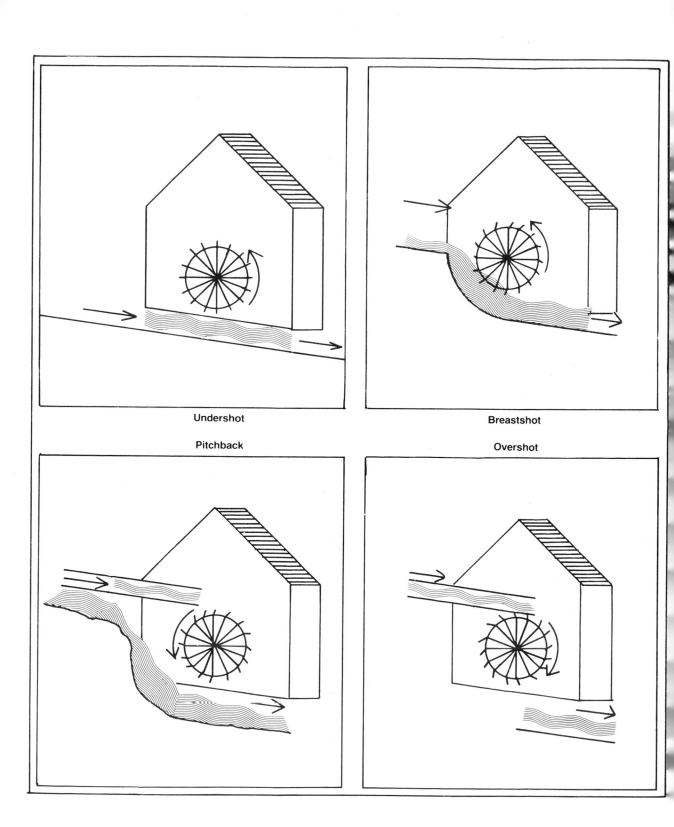

Undershot

Breastshot

Pitchback

Overshot

14. Diagram of types of Waterwheel.

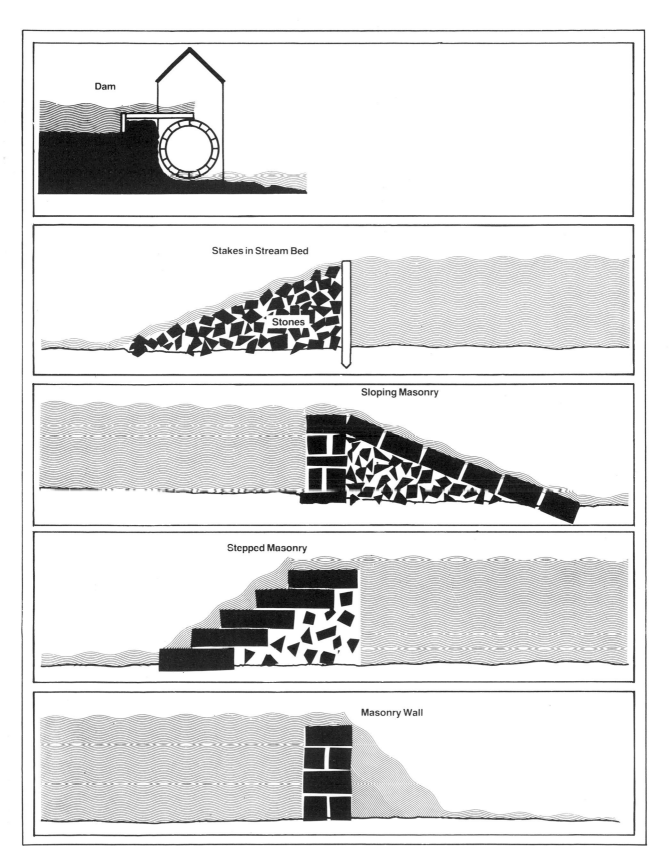

Dam

Stakes in Stream Bed

Stones

Sloping Masonry

Stepped Masonry

Masonry Wall

15. Diagram of types of Weir.

occurring during the late Anglo-Saxon or Viking occupations. Indeed, the acceptance of water power was so complete by the time of the compilation of the Domesday Book in 1086, that even mill sites, without a mill on them, had been allocated by the Saxon manors. Water rights were jealously guarded and controlled by manorial overlords in medieval England, as a useful source of income as well as being of importance to manorial industry. It was only the sparse population of the Pennine Dales, and hence a paucity of manorial settlements there, which enabled new textile mills to be established in such areas. There were few, if any, vacant sites suitable for water power in areas of substantial habitation.

The most primitive type of waterwheel known in Northern Europe is the Norse mill. This is a simple wheel lying in a horizontal plane. Water is directed from above onto a cluster of short vanes set at the bottom of a stout vertical axle. At the top of the axle is a pair of millstones, the lower one fixed, the upper one connected to the axle. As the water turns the vanes of the wheel, the axle turns the upper millstone without any intermediate gears. This type of waterwheel owes its name to the fact that it spread throughout Northern Europe, to become standard in Scandinavia. It remained the most characteristic form of water power in Sweden and Norway, and through colonisation by the Vikings it spread to Ireland, Scotland and the Scottish Isles. They must surely have introduced it also into Yorkshire, although no examples have survived here.

The Norse mill required sharply-falling water, such as a mountain or hillside stream (or an artificial leat) to turn the wheel by momentum. The vertically-mounted, undershot Roman mill, on the other hand, was better suited to more sluggish streams. The Norse waterwheel, though more primitive, was probably a later invention than the Roman waterwheel, and it seems likely that the two evolved independently.

The Roman writer, Vitruvius, whose great work, *De Architectura,* dates from *c.* 15 B.C., documents an undershot waterwheel with paddles, connected by an horizontal axle to a toothed pinion which interposed with a toothed gear wheel mounted on the vertical spindle driving the upper of a pair of millstones. The Roman type of undershot waterwheel and simple gearing remained virtually unchanged until the end of the medieval era, and is immediately recognisable as an ancestor of the—invariably static—machinery still to be found in some erstwhile corn watermills.

There are three main types of vertical waterwheel, appropriate to different topographical conditions. The simplest, and oldest, is the undershot wheel of the Roman mill. This has paddles which are moved by the kinetic energy of the flow of water. It utilises a slight fall of water, but requires a strong flow as the water has to move the weight of the wheel against gravity. Undershot wheels were usually found in mills powered by main rivers.

The next oldest form, and the most powerful, is the overshot wheel, motivated by the potential energy of falling water, which drops from above the wheel into the uppermost of the wheel's buckets, forcing them downwards by gravity. An overshot wheel can be powered by a very small amount of water, but it must be available at the level of the top of the wheel, perhaps from a high waterfall or a dam on a hillside. A pitchback wheel works very similarly to an overshot except that the wheel turns in the opposite direction. This has the advantage that the tail water then gets away better than from an overshot wheel, which may have problems of backwatering.

16

16. Model of a Norse Mill, formerly on display at the High Corn Mill Industrial and Folk Museum, Skipton.

17. Model of a Roman Mill, as described by Vitruvius, formerly on display at the High Corn Mill Industrial and Folk Museum, Skipton.

18. Undershot waterwheel at Brignall Mill near Barnard Castle. It is constructed almost entirely of wood, iron being used only for connecting the spokes to the rim, for bolts, on hoops around the axle, and for the gudgeons on which the waterwheel revolved. The water pushed onto the flat sides of the paddles, which are strengthened behind against this force. The ratchet wheel for raising and lowering the sluice gate can just be seen in the bottom left-hand corner.

19. Undershot waterwheel formerly in High Costa Mill near Pickering. It was constructed c. 1809 on the clasp-arm principle, the spokes clasping the axle, instead of being mortised radially into it.

20.   Overshot waterwheel at Newsham Mill near Barningham. To allow water to fall onto the wheel, the sluice was closed and a trapdoor opened. The situation was reversed for water to be discharged from the end of the pentrough. The mill was powered by small springs which were stored in a pond.

21.   Clasp-arm overshot waterwheel at Troutsdale Mill near Scarborough. Water was conveyed to the wheel in a wooden pentrough supported by the pillar on the right, and controlled by a sluice which could be worked from inside the mill, as the handle passed though the hole to the right of the window.

22. Hawes Mill in Wensleydale. The scar of an overshot waterwheel can be seen on the side of the building. It was fed by a wooden pentrough bringing water from the top of a waterfall a short distance upstream.

23. Bridge over the Duerley Beck at Hawes. In the spandrel of the bridge is a hole through which passed the pentrough to the mill, which is in the background on the left.

If the water meets the wheel at about the level of its axle, this is called a breastshot wheel; high-breastshot if just above axle-level; low breastshot if just below. The water falls into buckets, but the effect of gravity is lessened by the reduced height, and the wheel turns by a combination of the weight and the flow of water. It will thus be seen that the higher the fall of water available, the more efficient is the waterwheel. To increase the height, water was either collected into a dam built into a hillside, supplying a mill from above, or in flatter terrain, a weir was constructed across a river or stream, and the water taken from this artificially high level. Early weirs consisted of stakes driven into the river bed, packed with large boulders, which formed an effective wall across the river bed. Later weirs were usually of stone, either of sloping or straight section, or sometimes stepped. Where a river bed is falling, a watercourse was sometimes constructed to take water off at a higher level, and convey it with a minimum fall to a mill site lower down; by the time it reaches the mill it is at a much higher level than the river or stream at that point. An example of this is the mill at Gayle already described. The capital outlay in the earthworks involved, as well as the relative expense of the mill building and machinery, was one of the main reasons why mill sites were so jealously guarded.

The speed at which the wheel turns depends on the resistance offered by the machinery geared to it, and also on the speed of the flow of water. This can be regulated by a sluice placed immediately upstream of the wheel, which when closed stops water reaching the wheel, and when opened a little or a lot allows the wheel to turn slowly or fast. The power generated by a waterwheel depends on the fall of water, the flow of water, the width of the wheel, and its diameter—the last, on the lever principle, of moment equals the force multiplied by its distance from the fulcrum. Against these positive factors must be set the self-weight of the wheel, which obviously must be less than that needed to equalise the motive force available.

Early waterwheels tended to be narrow, were frequently undershot and generally inefficient. Until the early 17th century, waterwheels in Yorkshire were usually only able to operate one piece of machinery at a time, perhaps fulling stocks or one set of grinding stones. From that time, improved gearing and watercourse design enabled the water power to be used more economically. Two or more small waterwheels were frequently replaced by a single, larger wheel, connected to several machines by cog-wheels and shafts. From the 18th century, bevel gears were used to transmit power through 90 degrees from the waterwheel axle to the transmission shafts.

In the 18th and 19th centuries, great engineers such as John Smeaton, William Fairbairn and T. C. Hewes turned their attention to optimising available water power, under the stimulus of an increasing number of machines being produced which could utilise such power. The breastshot wheel was a development adopted in Yorkshire from the 17th century, which improved the efficiency of wheels on streams without sufficient fall for an overshot system. A great step forward in the amount of power which could be obtained from an undershot wheel was achieved by the French General Poncelet, who discovered that a 65 per cent. efficiency could be had from a mere fall of 5½ft. if an inclined sluice controlled the flow of water on to the wheel very accurately, and by replacing the flat paddles with scientifically-profiled buckets.

21

24. High breastshot waterwheel at Clifford, near Boston Spa, which drove a saw-mill. The axle, rim and buckets, which held the water, are of iron; only the spokes are of timber. The sluice on the right controlled the supply of water to the wheel from a dam across the road behind the wall. The gear-wheel behind the waterwheel sent power to the machinery.

Wheels and gearing were originally made entirely of wood. Iron was expensive and therefore used as sparingly as possible, only for the gudgeons on which the axle revolved, and clamps. A particular type of wood was used for each item of machinery: apple-wood, for example, was favoured for cogs, oak for the main frame of the wheel and the shaft, and elm for the floats of the wheel because of its resistance to rot.

Gradually improved processes enabled iron to be produced in larger, cheaper quantities, and wheels eventually became made entirely of iron. Wood was retained for some cog-teeth, as metal-to-wood was a quieter interaction than metal-to-metal. Wooden cogs also acted as a kind of fuse, in case anything drastic went wrong with the system, breaking sooner, and being easier to repair, than large sections of cast metal.

As the Industrial Revolution in Yorkshire gained momentum, waterwheels, which previously had only driven grinding stones, fulling stocks, tilt hammers and bellows, were required to motivate slubbing billies, carding engines, spinning frames and mules. As building construction became more industrialised, water-powered saw benches were introduced to handle far greater quantities of wood than had been possible with hand-sawing. Larger waterwheels were built, but this increased their self-weight, especially when they had to transmit power through a separate cogged 'pit' wheel attached to the same axle. To lighten the self-weight, the rim of the waterwheel itself was toothed, to drive gears directly without an intermediate pit wheel. The use of more iron allowed smaller sections of material to be used, which further decreased the self-weight. A few very light waterwheels were built, designed on the 'suspension' wheel principle used for bicycle wheels.

25. Low breastshot waterwheel in splendid isolation at Skelton, near Marske in Swaledale. It was built to generate electricity for Skelton Hall, but it is unlikely that a waterwheel, unlike a turbine, could have provided sufficient power.

23

26. Lendal Tower, part of the medieval walls of the city of York. It was used to house pumps supplying the city with water from the river Ouse, and was restored after the Victorian waterworks were built.

27. York Waterworks, Landing Lane, built in the 1870s. A steam engine in the building on the right powered the pumps.

28. Part of the 19th-century waterworks complex at York.

29. Buildings containing the filters, York Waterworks.

In the late 19th century, the more efficient water turbine took over from the wheel in many factories which retained water power. Cups enclosed within a casing are forced round at high speed by water falling from a considerable height. This, like the overshot wheel, required a greater fall than was commonly available, and the turbine never really caught on as a prime mover. However, it was, and still is, used to generate electricity. At Skelton, near Marske in Swaledale, is a waterwheel built to provide electricity for the Hall, but the installation was never completed.

Water is, of course, also an essential requirement for human settlements. The supply of water fit for drinking has exercised man's ingenuity since time immemorial. At Richmond in North Yorkshire, hollowed-out branches of elm trees were used to bring pure water into the town from springs outside during the reign of Queen Elizabeth I. About the same time, a waterwheel was first used to pump water from the river Ouse at York into the city. From 1682 this was replaced by a horse-gin situated in Lendal Tower, part of the medieval walls, and from the 18th century steam power was used. New waterworks were built outside the city itself in the 19th century. At Knaresborough, Castle Mill, an old corn mill, was converted to a waterworks in 1764, pumping water from the river Nidd up the side of the gorge into the town. In many areas, water towers were built to store water at a higher level than the settlements they served, water being pumped up by wind or steam power, and flowing down later by gravity. At first, the towers were built in brick, and later in the new material of reinforced concrete.

30. Pontefract Waterworks at Hensall, opened in 1933.

31. Hornsea: 19th-century water tower designed with polychromatic brickwork to imitate the Moorish style of architecture.

32. Goole: brick water tower of 1883 on the left, reinforced concrete water tower of 1926 on the right.

Wind

Wind power was introduced to Great Britain late in the 12th century. The earliest recorded evidence of the existence of a windmill is in Yorkshire, at Weedley in the East Riding, in 1185. Windmills were established in areas where there were no suitable streams or rivers to drive watermills, and the sites chosen were those exposed to the wind. Thus windmills are found on open sites, often on top of low hills. Even in ruined form, the remains of a windmill invariably present a dramatic profile to the viewer.

The earliest type of windmill was the post mill, which consisted of a stout wooden post set on large cross-beams, with other timbers bracing it into a vertical position. Mounted on the post was a small timber structure just large enough to contain a pair of grindstones and the simple machinery which connected them to the sails set on the front of the housing, and with a very small amount of space in which the miller might work. Access to the mill and its machinery was by means of a ladder, projecting from the small door at the back of the housing. From the rear also projected the strong tail-pole, which was used to push round the entire mill, by hand, so that the sails were turned into the wind. This arduous task was undertaken by the miller, who had also to carry sacks of corn up into the mill, and to bring down again the finished flour.

The carpenters who designed and built these post mills were extremely skilled craftsmen, for the structure had, by definition, to withstand strong winds. In addition, the mill had to be as light as possible for reasons of mobility, yet strong enough to remain level so that the machinery could work properly whichever way the mill was turned. The post mill housing was usually a timber-framed structure, to which was nailed timber boarding forming its walls.

No post mills now survive complete in Yorkshire, although there are some remains at East Cowick, and one survived at Little Smeaton, near Pontefract, until *c.* 1950. There were obviously quite a few examples near York, one of which, near Heslington, was recorded in 1826 by the Malton artist, George Nicholson. His sketch books, now in York City Art Gallery, also contain an illustration of a more advanced type of mill near Heworth, sketched in 1827. This drawing shows a small, fixed tower, probably in brick, with windows lighting its interior. The tower supports a cap and sails, both of which were turned into the wind by means of a tail-pole projecting from the back.

The tower mill superseded the post mill in the 17th century, and had many practical advantages. The tower was much more robust, being fixed, and could provide more accommodation. The superstructure alone—that is, the cap and sails—had to be turned into the wind, and because the tower itself rested on the ground, access was much easier. Sacks could be raised and lowered through trapdoors inside the mill by means of a hoist powered by the sails.

The tower of a windmill was always tapered, as the sails must not touch it when rotating. This caused design problems, as each successive course of masonry has to be slightly corbelled inwards over the one below. In some tower mills, the windows are irregularly spaced, to distribute these points of weakness around the structure, as in a windmill at Goole. Later mills, however, often have their windows in a line, such as the very tall, seven-storey example at Hessle, now in the shadow of the Humber Bridge. Sometimes windmills were raised in height, but in order to re-use the existing cap, the diameter of the new section had to stay the same instead of continuing the taper. This resulted in a windmill tower which appears to be craning at the neck.

Such a profile can be seen at Holgate windmill in the suburbs of York. The five-storey tower is built of brick, coated with bitumen to waterproof its inclined walls. It replaced a post mill about 1790, and had five sails, a rather unusual number, but one favoured by the great Yorkshire engineer, John Smeaton, who conducted experiments concerned with improving the efficiency of both water and wind power. Holgate Mill, although now minus its sails, has an ogee-shaped cap and, opposite the cross-shaft of the sails, a fantail, a device which automatically turned the sails, or sweeps, into the wind, a labour-saving improvement developed, like so many others, in the 18th century.

The only complete windmill in the county is at Skidby, near Beverley. This was built in 1821, and is preserved as a museum, being worked, and open to the public, on certain days each summer. Projecting from the tall, seven-storey tower is a balcony, just below the lowest point on the circumference of the four sails. From here the miller could adjust the shutters of each sweep according to the strength of the wind. The dramatic profile of this slender and elegant example of industrial architecture is a famous landmark, sitting atop a low hill in the rolling Wolds countryside.

33. 'Mill, between Heslington & York Feb. 7, 1826' sketched by George Nicholson of Malton (*York City Art Gallery*). This shows a post mill, already archaic in the early 19th century.

34. 'Mill, near Heworth Ap. 30, 1827' sketched by George Nicholson (*York City Art Gallery*). Tower mill, with tail-pole projecting from the back.

Only the towers of most windmills remain. Some continued in use until relatively recently by having supplementary steam power, as at Lelley, near Bridlington. Here the tower retains the cross and windshaft of the sails, and the framework of the fantail. Close by is the chimney for the steam engine, the boiler of which also survives. Many windmill towers are now simply abandoned. A few have been converted into cottages, and one at Askham Bryan, again near York, where the topography of the Vale of York is so suitable for wind power, now supports a water tank, a sensible new use for a redundant structure.

Wind power was primarily used in Yorkshire for grinding corn, but was also used for crushing chalk, as at Hessle, and to drive pumps for drainage purposes. In contrast to the large towers already described, in a garden at Elvington there is a small, ivy-covered brick tower which formerly supported a wind-pump used to drain water from a nearby brickworks in the flat basin of the river Derwent.

35. Windmill tower at Goole. The windows were offset in plan to avoid lines of weakness in the structure.

36. Very tall windmill tower at Hessle. The length of the sails can be calculated from the scars of the balcony, the doorway to which is visible.

37. Holgate Windmill, York. Built about 1790 to replace a post mill, it had five sails. The tower is of brick, darkened with bitumen, and has been heightened. Note the ogee shape of the cap.

38. Askham Bryan Windmill, near York, used to support a water tank.

39. Skidby Windmill, near Beverley. The only windmill in Yorkshire which still retains its sails. It was built in 1821. The fantail, on the left, responds to any changes in wind direction by turning the sails to catch the wind. The bottom of the sails just reaches to the balcony.

32

40. Windmill at Lelley, near Bridlington, showing the cross and windshaft of the sails, and framework of the fantail.

41. Windmill at Lelley, near Bridlington, showing the chimney and boiler of the steam engine which supplemented the wind power.

Steam

The steam engine was conceived in the south-west of England, in 1698, when a Devonian, Thomas Savery, a captain in the Royal Engineers, invented a steam pump which could extract water out of mine-shafts. Shortly afterwards, in 1708, Thomas Newcomen, a Dartmouth blacksmith, produced the first beam engine. Use of this device quickly spread throughout the areas already engaged in mining operations, including Yorkshire. The Newcomen engine consisted primarily, as the term 'beam-engine' implies, of a horizontal timber beam, which rocked about a central point of support. Attached to one end was a vertical cylinder inside which a piston rod could move up and down. Shots of steam forced up the piston, which dropped back down by gravity in between when the pressure was reduced by condensing the steam with cold water. At the other end of the beam hung another vertical rod, moving down and up as the other piston worked, which pumped water up from the mine-shaft.

The Newcomen engine used a lot of coal because the cylinder was heated up then cooled down each time. However, this hardly mattered if it was used at a coal mine. The use of such steam-powered pumps enabled deeper shafts to be sunk for coal-mining purposes. The demand for coal was growing in the early 18th century, both for industrial use, and also for domestic purposes as supplies of firewood were increasingly exhausted.

At Elsecar, near Barnsley, there survives a Newcomen-type engine preserved by the National Coal Board, and which is gradually being restored. The engine house at Elsecar bears the date 1787, although the atmospheric engine there dates from 1795. It is typical of early beam-engine houses in being a tall, narrow structure, and is some-what reminiscent of those famous engine houses associated with the Cornish tin-mines, although they usually have a more prominent single chimney than the two small chimneys at Elsecar which are almost domestic in character. Indeed, the whole engine-house borrows from Georgian architecture, as do many early industrial buildings. The timber beam had to be replaced in cast-iron *c.* 1836, though the engine-house itself wore better, and continued to support the beam's rocking motion until *c.* 1930.

In the second half of the 18th century, after a gap of many years without any major developments, James Watt made the steam engine more economical in its use of coal by condensing the steam in a separate chamber, thus allowing the cylinder to stay hot all the time, and later he powered the downward movement of the piston, so that it acted positively in both directions, thus doubling its efficiency. At this stage, however, the beam engine was only suitable for pumping, as it produced a reciprocating motion. As well as pumping water out of underground shafts, early beam-engines were also used to pump up water from rivers to supply towns and cities, and in some cases to pump a small supply of water on to the top of one of the larger waterwheels being built to drive the first textile mills.

The next step was to adapt the steam engine to the rotary action needed for driving machines. The simplest way of doing this was by using a crank, but there were problems with the patent concerning that idea. So Watt developed a 'sun and planet' system: the 'planet' was a cogged wheel on the opposite end of the beam to the cylinder. This travelled round a larger, cogged 'sun' on the axle of a flywheel which it thus rotated.

42. Elsecar, near Barnsley. Newcomen-type steam engine used to pump water out of a coal mine from *c.*1787. Note the contemporary colliery housing in the background.

43. Elsecar, near Barnsley. Rear view of engine house, dated 1787, the design borrowed from Georgian domestic architecture.

44. Crank Mill, Morley. A fulling mill, which had one of the earliest beam engines with a crank to produce rotary power.

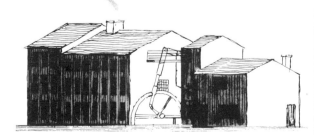

45. A 19th-century engraving showing the use of both traction and stationary steam engines for quarrying in the Yorkshire Dales.

46. Horizontal steam engine on display in Bradford Industrial Museum.

It was towards the end of the 18th century before beam-engines were fitted with cranks. One of the earliest-known examples of such an engine was installed about 1790 in Morley, at a fulling mill which took its name from the strange device—Crank Mill. The beam protruded through the engine house, as at Elsecar, but on the lower end of the external vertical rod was a short crank connected to the axle of a large flywheel which was also situated outside, on the narrow end of the main mill building. From here, drives were taken through into the mill interior. The mill finally closed down in 1979.

As well as driving items of machinery in factories, steam engines with rotary action could also be used for winding cages up and down collieries, and for winding wagons of coal or other heavy materials up inclines ready for transportation to further destinations. Towards the end of the 19th century, rotative beam engines were extensively used for pumping water from one direction, and sewerage towards another, as towns and cities improved their water supply and sanitation. It should also be mentioned that not all steam engines were stationary; in the late 19th century traction engines played a large part in industrial transport and in agriculture. A 19th-century engraving showing quarrying operations in the Yorkshire Dales shows the use of both stationary and traction steam engines.

From the early 19th century, steam engines were able to work under a higher pressure of steam, and were thus more powerful. Some engines had two cylinders, one working under high pressure, the second utilising the lower, but nevertheless still potent, pressure of steam leaving the first cylinder: this was called a compound engine. Later, a third cylinder was added, on the same principle, forming a triple expansion engine.

By the mid 19th century, the supremacy of the beam engine was overtaken by the horizontal engine, in which the cylinder was placed horizontally, and the beam was replaced by a connecting rod. For the last phase of the steam engine's era, the cylinder was returned to a vertical position, but its previous arrangement was inverted, and the cylinders were lifted above the crankshaft. High-speed engines of this type were used in steamships, and also for generating electricity, until being superseded by steam turbines, in which small blades were forced round by high-pressure steam instead of the high-pressure water which drove water turbines.

The increasing pressure and size requirements of steam engines necessitated the production of increasingly efficient boilers. In the early days, engines and boilers had frequently exploded. The first boilers were small containers which took their names from popular shapes, e.g., 'haystack' or 'wagon' types. The first person successfully to build a high-pressure boiler was Richard Trevithick, who invented the Cornish boiler in 1812. This was a large cylindrical container, set sideways. In 1844, the even larger Lancashire boiler was developed by William Fairbairn of Manchester.

In the early days of steam power, when a lot of coal was used, but relatively little power generated, it was essential to have good access to coal. The phenomenal expansion of Bradford is an excellent illustration of the advantage gained by cheap coal. In the late 18th century, when newly-developed textile machines required water power to drive the early mills, Bradford was at a disadvantage, having but insignificant supplies of water. However, from the turn of the 19th century, as steam power began to be used more extensively, Bradford grew rapidly, because the town had access to coal, and also to iron for building steam engines and other machines, and in addition had excellent building stone with which to erect new mills. Horsfall's Mill at North Wing, Bradford, dating from *c.* 1820, is one of the oldest mills in the area.

The development of more powerful steam engines, and the opening of railway lines along which coal could be cheaply transported, enabled the building of more and larger factories. Bradford can boast many huge mills, one of the most impressive being Lister's Mill at Manningham, with a correspondingly large and Italianate mill chimney. Legend claims improbably that a carriage and horses could be driven around its top, without mentioning a method of raising them to the top for the purpose!

The last generation of steam-powered factories was, inevitably, the largest. Their enormously tall chimneys are now frequently sentenced to demolition as unsafe. The size of those remaining is often difficult to comprehend, particularly as they are in scale with the vast mill buildings which they served. At Dean Clough Mills, Halifax, there is the tallest stone chimney in Europe, almost 100m. high, built in 1857. At the top is a crown of cast-iron plates, giving it the name 'Corona chimney'. By the late 19th century, many industrial towns had forests of huge factory chimneys, belching out filthy smoke, and creating the 'dark, satanic mills' image of northern Britain.

Factory life entirely depended on the steam engine, and the ponderously-turning god was placated by being cosseted and polished, and housed in a luxurious temple. Much of this was, of course, also practical. The moving parts of the engine were lovingly cleaned, polished and oiled in order for them to move with as little friction as possible, but this does not explain the habit of giving the engine a name, usually feminine. The engine-houses were kept immaculately clean in order for the engine to be kept clean. The foundations of the engine-houses had to be enormously strong to withstand the rapid vibrations of a huge engine, but this does not explain the decorative tiles and panelling often found there.

47. Horsfall's Mill, North Wing, Bradford. Dating from *c.*1820, it was one of the first steam-powered textile mills, and one of Bradford's oldest industrial buildings.

One of the outstanding examples of a luxurious engine house is at Holbeck, in Leeds, where stands a factory called Tower Works. It was built in 1864 for the manufacture of components for carding and combing machines for the textile industry, and its mill chimney was a copy, by the Leeds architect, Thomas Shaw, of the great Lamberti tower in Verona, in Italy, which gave the works its name. The engine-house below was designed to be a tribute to the great names of textile history, and portrait medallions of men such as Arkwright and Heilmann, by the sculptor, Alfred Drury, are set into the once-gleaming white tiles lining the building. Such was the authority of the engineer in charge of such vital equipment, that the elderly managing director still remembered vividly how, as a small boy, the grandson of the then owner, even he was not allowed to go in and watch the engine until his hands had been inspected to see if they were clean!

The firm's penchant for distinctive industrial architecture continued, and in 1899 it installed a dust extraction plant to cope with the steel filings emitted into the factory during production. The filings were collected and resold for the manufacture of 'sparklers' for Bonfire Night! The tower to give the necessary up-draught for the extraction was designed by another local architect, William Bakewell, and based on another famous Italian landmark, the campanile of Florence Cathedral designed by Giotto, in brilliant white and coloured marble. The Holbeck version is in brick, with only one stage of 'openings' formed in gilded tiles. The ledges, however, make a useful nesting place for one of Leeds' pairs of kestrels.

By the late 19th century, the steam engine had become ubiquitous, present even in many small workshops as a labour-saving device. Some larger farms had one to power threshing machines, and at Baldersby Grange, near Ripon, the Home Farm had a steam engine which also served the estate laundry.

48. Chimney for steam engine at Pickering, built after the opening of the railway.

49. Lister's Mill, Manningham, Bradford: one of the largest textile mills in West Yorkshire, being over ¼ mile in length.

50. Lister's Mill, Manningham, Bradford: Italianate detailing visible on the end of one of the two parallel blocks.

51. Lister's Mill, Manningham, Bradford: The steam engine chimney takes the form of a detached Italianate campanile, over 60m high.

52.   Lister's Mill, Manningham, Bradford: the top of the chimney, showing the inscription *BUILT A.D. 1872.3*   (Photo: *Alan Wilcox*)

53. Dean Clough Mills, Halifax. The corona chimney, built in 1857, is almost 100m tall, and reputedly the largest stone-built chimney in Europe.

54. Tower Works, Holbeck, Leeds: a general view.

55. Tower Works, Holbeck, Leeds: steam engine chimney of 1864, copied from the Lamberti Tower in Verona.

56. Tower Works, Holbeck, Leeds: chimney of dust extraction plant of 1899, copied from Giotto's Campanile, Florence.

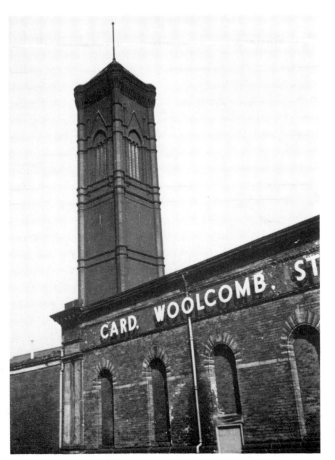

57. Meanwood Road, Leeds, looking towards Sheepscar. Late 19th-century factories, with enormous steam-engine chimneys. Compare them with the parked car. Note the back-to-back terraced housing nearby, and the mid-20th century equivalent, the tower blocks, behind.

58. Baldersby Grange near Ripon. Water tower, to which water was pumped by a steam engine also serving the Home Farm and estate laundry.

Gas

Candles and oil-lamps were considered extremely dangerous forms of artificial lighting for industrial premises, and the first factories were designed to maximise available daylight. Early industrial buildings usually had evenly-spaced windows, and were fairly narrow from the front to back, so that daylight reached to the middle of each floor from the windows on either side. The hours when work was possible inevitably varied with the time of year—as it had done when most people were engaged in agriculture—and people could therefore earn less in winter than in summer. This was obviously a less than ideal situation for the workforce, but what was of greater importance to the owner was the fact that machines stood idle for much of the time.

As more machines were developed, and as the sources of motive power were improved to drive larger numbers of machines, there was more incentive to keep the factories working longer hours. Return on investment in machines and steam engines would be maximised if a shift system could be introduced so that the factory was productive right round the clock.

The first commercial production of coal-gas was begun by William Murdoch in 1798 for lighting Boulton and Watt's Soho factory in Birmingham. Within a few years, Boulton and Watt were supplying gas-making plants to textile mills. The next step was to produce gas for lighting the streets of the growing towns. Ironically, one of the first Yorkshire towns to have a gasworks was Richmond, a historic borough and not one of the rapidly-expanding industrial centres, where the number of strangers moving in looking for work made street-lighting particularly desirable. As most towns gained gaslighting, places of public entertainment increasingly tempted people out during the evenings, to spend some of the money they earned in the factories. Large public buildings, including theatres and, later, music halls, were lighted by gas, and gaslighting has become inextricably associated with our image of Victorian life.

59. Gas-Works, Kirkbymoorside, an impressive advertisement for cast-iron shop-fronts made by a local foundry.

60. Whitby: Gas-Works alongside the railway line.

61. Bridlington: gasholder with Victorian cast-ironwork.

62. Howden Gas-Works, with a small gasholder behind. The plaque records the date of erection as 1832, and of enlargement in 1864. The influence of Georgian architecture may still be detected in the pediment containing the plaque, and the arched entrance, originally open.

63. Howden Gas-Works, and manager's house. The building survived because it continued in use as a Gas Board Showroom after the conversion to natural gas.

64. Beverley Gas-Works: imposing gateway dated 1825, with a classical arch set within a Tuscan entablature. Note the cast-iron gates.

65. Beverley Gas-Works: inside the gateway, the buildings were more utilitarian, but still pleasing. This little building housed a blacksmith's forge, where the retorts and other equipment could be repaired. Note the louvred ventilator.

In those towns with a public gas supply, gaslight replaced oil-lamps and candles, and from the middle of the 19th century gas was also used for cooking and for heating water, and later for gas fires. Although gas was not extensively used as a form of industrial motive power, it made a notable contribution to the social and economic progress of the Industrial Revolution. As it was something of a status symbol for a town to have gaslit streets, the gasworks often reflected municipal pride. At Howden the building was dated, and at Beverley an impressive Tuscan classical order graced the gateway. A fine cast-iron shop-front advertised the product of a nearby foundry at Kirkbymoorside. As gaslight was mainly required during the evenings, and as it was sensible to produce the gas during the normal working day, it was necessary to store it. For this purpose, the gasholder was developed. Most were cylindrical tanks, held vertically within a cast-iron frame. The largest buildings at a gasworks housed the retorts—large pipes in which coal was heated. There was, of course, a by-product from the manufacture of coal-gas—coke—which itself occupies a place in the history of fuels. Gasworks were often built beside the railway lines which brought their supplies of coal, as at Whitby. Railway stations were usually lighted by gas, and at Richmond the station had its own little gas-plant, because the station was across the river from the town and the local gas supply.

66. Richmond Railway Station: small gas house supplying the station complex alone. The chimney has been demolished, but remains of the retorts are still inside the building. Note the raised louvred section of roof, a typical characteristic of retort sheds.

Few industries can have experienced such a rapid demise as that of the manufacture of town gas. The discovery of natural gas under the North Sea caused the closure of gasworks within the short space of the decade of the 1960s. As the industry had been nationalised, there was a central policy of demolishing redundant gas-making plants, unlike the buildings of privately-owned industrial concerns, which tend to lie derelict after they have closed. Not many gasworks buildings survive. On one or two sites, some buildings were retained as showrooms for gas appliances and offices for the collection of payments, as at Howden in East Yorkshire. However, such small offices have been closed during subsequent 'rationalisation' and the gasmen now cometh from only a few depots, often at considerable distances from their customers.

Gas appliances are no longer the monopoly of the gas boards, and are sold by the larger domestic retailers of other goods. In most places, only a solitary gasholder, storing a small quantity of gas to allow for fluctuations in demand, serves as a reminder of an erstwhile industry.

67. York Gas-Works: gasholder with Victorian cast-ironwork.

68. York Gas-Works: pump house of *c.*1885.

69. York Gas-Works: retort shed just before demolition — the original louvred roof has been replaced.

70. York Gas-Works: brick detailing of *c.*1885.

71. Pocklington: a more utilitarian gasholder.

72. Driffield: cast-iron gasholder.

Electricity

By the end of the 19th century, most towns of any size were considering the construction of a power station, using coal-fired steam engines to generate electricity. A site suitable for a power station needed to be alongside a railway line, in order to be supplied with coal, and also adjacent to a river, for water was used to cool, and thus condense, the steam produced, and this water in turn had also to be cooled. The condensation was effected by cooling towers, which acted like oversized chimneys. At first these were constructed of timber, and examples survived at Bradford and Hull as late as the 1970s. Valley Road Power Station in Bradford, alongside the valley-bottom railway lines, had several impressive groups of wooden cooling towers, square in plan, and tapering slightly towards the top. Built in 1898, they gave over seventy years of service, despite the timber being constantly saturated with steam.

Reinforced concrete superseded timber as the main building material for cooling towers in the early 20th century, and we are now more familiar with the groups of circular, elegantly-waisted funnels of the modern power stations which serve the National Grid instead of a specific town. Many of these are clustered to the south of the Vale of York, such as that at Drax, convenient for deliveries from the Yorkshire coalfield.

73. Hull: wooden cooling towers of *c.*1900, and later reinforced concrete version. Note the position alongside the railway line.

Municipal power stations, although fairly utilitarian in character, were usually monumental in scale and an emblem of civic pride. York power station still has a tall chimney of elegant profile which is a landmark from many parts of the city, particularly from the bar walls. Built in 1900, it still bears traces of the camouflage paint applied to factory chimneys during the Second World War as a deterrent to the recognition of such a landmark by crews of enemy aircraft.

In rural areas, particularly the Yorkshire Dales, those rivers and streams which had powered corn watermills were often put to good use once more generating electricity for their village from a turbine, installed in place of the waterwheel. Batteries were charged during the day to provide power, mainly for lighting, in the evening. Mills at Newsham, Wensley, Askrigg, Reeth and Harome, among others, were used in this way. Some working corn mills still generate electricity from their own turbine to work modern milling machinery.

74. Wooden cooling towers, Valley Road Power Station, Bradford, *c.*1898. (MG)

75. Drax Power Station, built to burn coal from the Yorkshire coalfield.

76. York Power Station. A utilitarian brick structure, but Portland stone is used for decorative details.

77. York Power Station. Elegant chimney of 1900, still bearing traces of Second World War camouflage paint.

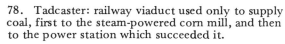

78. Tadcaster: railway viaduct used only to supply coal, first to the steam-powered corn mill, and then to the power station which succeeded it.

79. Tadcaster: steam-powered corn mill of 1883, converted to a coal-fired power station in 1903, and now used as a bonded warehouse.

80. Harome: old corn mill, now with a turbine generating electricity from water power.

81. Hydro-electric power station at Linton Lock.

At Tadcaster, the steam-powered corn mill on the site of the manorial watermill was transformed into a coal-fired power station by the local brewery, John Smith's, in 1903, to supply the brewery and the town with electricity. It is a neo-Romanesque building adjacent to the railway viaduct put across the river Wharfe to carry a new railway line between York and Leeds. Completion of the line was halted by the collapse of the York and North Midland Railway Company in 1849. However, the viaduct served to bring coal first to the mill, and then to the power station, from the existing line between Tadcaster and Wetherby. The power station closed in the 1950s when Tadcaster was supplied by the National Grid, and it is now used as a bonded warehouse by the brewery. A shorter-lived scheme was that to generate hydro-electric power from the fall of water at Linton Lock on the river Ouse north of York.

82. Corporation Mills, Sowerby Bridge alongside Rochdale Canal. (MG)

III

TRANSPORT DEVELOPMENTS

General Introduction

THE PROCESS OF INDUSTRIALISATION was heavily dependent on good communications, for in order to specialise in a particular product, it is essential to be able to reach markets further afield than just those nearby. Thus transport facilities are necessary to distribute, or 'export', goods. Although some industries used raw materials obtainable close at hand, others also had to 'import' their ingredients. The advent of steam power additionally focused attention on communications, for few areas had coal available on their doorsteps, and only places near a canal or railway line could obtain coal in sufficient quantities, and at a reasonable enough price, to make steam power a viable proposition.

Any transport system requires a high level of organisation, as it needs co-operation between two or more communities. The expenditure of effort for the common cause is greater than the extent of the return for any one individual. The Romans, being a military people, had such a high level of organisation and, when the Roman army was withdrawn from Britain early in the fifth century, their famous network of roads remained unsurpassed until the 19th century. Without centralised supervision, these roads went generally unmaintained, and gradually deteriorated in the ensuing centuries, although they formed the basis of our trunk road system until the start of the motorway era.

One of the main problems of road transport has always been the cost of building bridges. As bridges constitute the most obvious architectural expression of road transport, they are dealt with at some length in this section. Settlements along navigable rivers have always used them for transport, and throughout history the skills of craftsmen involved in building boats for use on rivers, and even seaworthy ships, have consistently maintained an average degree of technological sophistication higher than in any comparable field. In the late 17th century, the climate of economic thought which eventually grew into the Industrial Revolution resulted in the improvement of some rivers. However, it was to be another half century and more before brand new waterways were cut, outstripping the road system, whose turnpike trusts had in the main sought to improve existing roads, rather than building new ones.

Both turnpike and navigation companies required an Act of Parliament to operate, but slowly they learnt the benefits—and cost—of taking an overall view of a stretch of road or water, instead of dealing with short lengths. However, they still worked independently with their own individual standards, including the size of locks and thus of craft, so that goods had to be transferred from the boats of one canal company to those of another to continue their journey. Although some trusts and companies commissioned purpose-built structures of some considerable architectural

59

merit, neither the turnpike roads nor the canals contributed anything like as much to architectural development as did the railway companies.

With the railway companies came a change of scale and style of operation. They at last achieved some standardisation over the whole country, for instance of track gauge, and even the adoption of Greenwich Mean Time throughout the country can be credited to them, since it enabled timetables to be operated nationwide. Railway stations may be seen as one of the few entirely new types of transport architecture. Canal warehouses developed from older types of storage building, and their technology was shared with the buildings of other industries; but the passenger station, designed to tempt the man in the street inside, was an original innovation. In station buildings, the railway companies discovered the value of architecture as a tool of public relations. They made a determined attempt to attract custom by establishing a reputable image with fine buildings. No industry has wooed the public so assiduously, with grand architecture as the free gift. The second generation of railway buildings expressed the technological achievement of the mid-19th century, as epitomised by the railway system, particularly in their fine roof spans.

Roads

In the Middle Ages, travelling by road was a hazardous business. The highways were badly rutted, hard and dusty in summer, wet and boggy in winter, and often passed through forests which gave good cover for highwaymen. Such were the dangers that chapels were built in strategic locations for travellers to give thanks for a safe passage thus far accomplished, and to pray for similar good fortune on the next stage of the journey. In some cases the chapel was on the bank near a bridge; in others it was on the bridge itself, as at Wakefield. There, in the middle of the nine-arched medieval bridge, is the 14th-century chapel endowed in 1398 as a chantry for prayer for his and other Christian souls by Edmund, Duke of York. The chapel, in the Decorated style of Gothic architecture, was heavily restored in 1847 by Sir George Gilbert Scott.

83. Chantry Chapel on the medieval bridge at Wakefield.

Various attempts were made to improve the medieval road network, generally with little success. In the 16th century, in the aftermath of the upheaval caused by the dissolution of the monasteries, the 1555 Act for the Amending of Highways devolved to the ubiquitous unit of Tudor administration, the parish, the unenviable responsibility for maintaining those sections of main roads within its boundaries. Each parish had to elect two Surveyors of Highways, who had the invidious task of exacting four days of Statute Labour from each householder. The Surveyors' unpopularity must have been increased in 1563 when another Statute of Highways increased the requirement to six days. Needless to say, more prosperous householders paid some unfortunate to go in their stead, while the poor went reluctantly, and did as little work as they could get away with. This unskilled labour was capable only of clearing out ditches or filling in potholes with rubble; it could effect no profound improvements.

A less irksome piece of legislation passed in 1712 required that travellers should know the direction of the nearest market towns. Two dated examples of stones giving this information are illustrated here. The first is situated opposite to one of the carriage drive entrances to Danby Hall in Wensleydale, still the seat of the ancient Scrope family. The stone, which is five-sided, has on the four rear faces the names of local market towns—Bedale, Ripon, Richmond and Leyburn—but on the front is a bit of self-advertisement—'The Road To SIMON SCROOP Esqr. of Danby 1712'. A contemporary guide stone a few miles away, at some crossroads along the Ripon–Bedale road, shows the direction to Richmond.

84. Guide stone showing the direction of local market towns outside the entrance to Danby Hall in Wensleydale.

85. Guide stone near Bedale giving directions at a cross-roads.

61

During medieval times, and indeed later, the main unit of transport was the pack-animal—pony, mule or horse—a sure-footed beast which carried goods in two paniers hung on to a wooden saddle. The animals were fastened together in a train, with a human 'jagger' in charge of them at the front. The pack-animals picked their way very successfully over rugged terrain, nimbly climbing up hill and dropping down dale. Their only disadvantage was that they could not carry large quantities of heavy commodities such as coal or lead.

On well-used routes, small bridges were built to enable the ponies to cross streams more easily, not for their comfort, but to ensure that their cargo did not get wet if the animal lost its footing in the stream bed. Most true 'pack-horse' bridges were built very economically, providing only a narrow path crossing the stream in a characteristic steep curve, and without parapets. To enclose the animal plus its packs between parapets would have required a much larger bridge structure. Most pack-horse bridges have had parapets added to them since they have become used mainly as footbridges. At Thornthwaite in Nidderdale an old pack-horse bridge used stone slabs for both the parapet walls and the paving.

One of the most elegant bridges, in a beautiful setting, is at Ivelet in Swaledale, where the bridge, built in the late 16th century, makes a single leap, reminiscent of the grace of a ballet dancer, over the river Swale. Although narrow by modern standards, it was wide for its time. Its predecessor was on the Corpse Way, along which the medieval inhabitants of upper Swaledale had to carry their dead on a long journey down to the parish church at Grinton for burial. A large stone at the north end of Ivelet Bridge was used to rest the heavy wicker baskets.

At Sowerby near Thirsk is another, narrow single-span bridge, dating from *c*. 1672. A plaque on the old bridge at Hebden Bridge in the Calder Valley states that it was built *c*. 1510, replacing a timber bridge. It provided a river crossing on an important pack-horse route leading steeply down from the historic hill-top settlement of Heptonstall. Eventually, at the start of the Industrial Revolution, a new settlement grew up on the river, and took its name from the Hebden Bridge. The bridge has two arches, separated by a vast cutwater.

Streams and narrow rivers could be bridged by a single span, with both the abutments resting on dry land. Over a wider river, several arches were needed, and the piers in between had to be built into the river bed. To do this, and to allow the mortar to set, it is necessary to build a coffer-dam to hold back or divert the flow of the river, preferably at low water. This complex and costly operation was beyond the scope of smaller towns, and there were relatively few bridges crossing major rivers until the new materials and techniques of the Industrial Revolution both increased the demand for transport routes, and also made bridge-building easier.

Few old bridges survive, most having been rebuilt in the 19th century after decades of frustration as the old structure repeatedly needed repair, especially after floods. The North Bridge over the river Ure at Ripon is a medieval structure with six arches, mostly of different dates, the bridge having been repaired piecemeal over the centuries. Higher up Wensleydale is Kilgram Bridge, built for the Cistercian monks of Jervaulx Abbey. Typically of monastic achievements, their bridge-building was much more sophisticated than that of their lay contemporaries, and the four segmental arches look quite modern in profile. Underneath, however, are ribs, a medieval bridge-

86. Pack-horse Bridge at Thornthwaite in Nidderdale.

87. Ivelet Bridge makes a graceful leap over the river Swale.

88. Narrow bridge of *c.*1672 at Sowerby near Thirsk.

89. Hebden Bridge, which gave its name to a settlement.

90. North Bridge, Ripon, with medieval and later arches.

91. Kilgram Bridge, built by the monks of Jervaulx Abbey.

92. Wensley Bridge, with two medieval arches.

building technique derived from vaulting Gothic cathedrals. Not far away, at Wensley, the present bridge incorporates two arches of the medieval structure. Crossing the lower reaches of the river Swale is the bridge at Topcliffe, which consists of the old ribbed structure of 1622, later widened on the upstream side.

The medieval rib system of bridge-building was also used when the bridge was rebuilt in 1562 at Boroughbridge, another town which takes its name from the bridge serving the much older settlement at Aldborough. This bridge was widened, and partly rebuilt in 1784, by Blind Jack Metcalf of Knaresborough, a remarkable character who, despite his disability, made important strides in improving the techniques of road-construction in the 18th century.

93. Topcliffe Bridge, where the old ribbed structure, nearest the camera, has been widened by the addition of a new bridge alongside.

The repair of what timber and stone-built bridges existed, let alone the construction of new ones, was quite beyond the unskilled capabilities of a parish labour force, and by the early 17th century the county authorities had to assume responsibility for the most essential bridges. Several had to be rebuilt, such as that at Ulshaw in Wensleydale, already mentioned. Another 17th-century bridge (dated 1650) crosses the river Derwent at Kexby. There are three arches in all, including one on dry land, divided by triangular cutwaters. Each arch has three chamfered orders, which serve to widen out the carriageway over the basic structure. The bridge was so important that when in the 18th century turnpike roads were being promoted, the new roads terminated at the bridge. The Act of Parliament for the Beverley–Kexby Bridge turnpike road was passed in 1764, and that for the York–Kexby Bridge–Garrowby Hill turnpike road in 1765. The bridge has now been bypassed, and is no longer maintained by the highways authority.

94. Boroughbridge Bridge of 1562 and 1784.

95. Details of ribs of 1562 underneath Boroughbridge Bridge.

96. Kexby Bridge over the river Derwent, built in 1650, but now obsolete and falling into disrepair.
97. Bridge over the river Derwent at Stamford Bridge, designed by York architect William Etty in 1727.

The movement towards the provision of more and better bridges continued throughout the 18th century, responding to the needs of greater industrial activity, and also social requirements, as people travelled about more, particularly to those towns and cities such as Richmond and York which became important centres of fashionable activities in Georgian times. Georgian architectural influence is very noticeable in the design of 18th-century bridges. The York architect, William Etty, who was probably responsible for that city's Mansion House, designed a new crossing over the river Derwent at Stamford Bridge in 1727. The central segmental arch is elegantly flanked by two semi-circular arches, one of which spans the lock built when the navigation on the Derwent was improved in 1701.

At West Tanfield, the bridge over the river Ure, built in 1734, has a plaque on it which marked the 'Diversion of the North and West Ridings'. It has three segmental arches separated by cutwaters which have concave curving tops. An extremely decorative bridge was built *c.* 1775 at Scampston, carrying the A64 between Malton and Scarborough. It has three rusticated arches, and an elegant balustraded parapet.

During the 18th century, counties began to appoint specialist bridgemasters, a position held for both the North and West Ridings by the great York architect, John Carr, who, as a result, was responsible for the design of innumerable handsome bridges, including that at Skipton-on-Swale, built in 1781.

98.   The bridge over the river Ure at West Tanfield, which marks the boundary of the old North and West Ridings of Yorkshire.

99. Scampston Bridge of *c.*1775, with rusticated arches and balustraded parapet.

100. Skipton-on-Swale Bridge of 1781, by John Carr of York.

By the early 19th century, there was additional emphasis on engineering considerations, as well as elegance. The old Ouse Bridge at York was a hump-backed medieval structure with a chapel, gaol, houses and shops on it, and for centuries it had been a cause of worry. The competition for the design of a replacement was won by the York architect, Peter Atkinson, junior. The new bridge was built between 1810–20, the long period of time taken being partly due to the need to retain the old one in use. The new bridge was built in two halves lengthwise, the first half being constructed alongside the old bridge, which was only taken down when the new half was completed, and the second half was then built. The join can still be seen underneath the three segmental arches, which provide an almost level profile for the carriageway.

Such were the manifold problems of constructing bridges that Ouse Bridge remained the only river crossing even for so important a city as York until 1863, when Lendal Bridge was opened. It was built in response to an increase in traffic in the area of the old railway station of 1841.

The Industrial Revolution produced new ways of using iron which had profound implications for bridge-building. Ironbridge in Shropshire takes its name from the oldest surviving (1779) and most famous example of its type. Although documentary evidence exists of an earlier iron bridge in Yorkshire, made by the Leeds ironmonger, Maurice Tobin in 1768, for Sir George Armytage of Kirklees Hall, it has not survived. Other experiments with the new technology were also short-lived.

The surviving early suspension bridges in Wales by the great Scottish engineer, Thomas Telford, over the Menai Straits and the river Conway, both opened in 1826, are rightly famous. Only three years later a suspension bridge was built over the river Ure near Middleham, designed by architects Hansom and Welch. The pylons are castellated, and the iron cables passed into them through loopholes. Unfortunately, the design was not technically satisfactory, and the new bridge failed within a year or two of completion because, it is said, a herd of cattle crossing over the bridge fell into step, and caused vibrations which the suspension structure could not withstand. By 1864 a new cast-iron carriageway had been put in position, although the idiosyncratic castellated pylons remain. One hopes that the Humber Bridge, which was when built the world's longest clear-span suspension bridge, will last somewhat longer!

It was not only suspension bridges which failed. Lendal Bridge, the second road bridge to span the Ouse at York, collapsed during construction in 1861, killing six workmen. The lattice girders, which had been designed by William Dredge, were literally dredged out of the river and taken to Scarborough, where they were used in 1865 to form the famous suicide spot, the Valley Bridge. A fresh attempt was made at building Lendal Bridge, to a new design by Thomas Page, engineer of Westminster Bridge in London. This time the venture was successful, and the bridge opened within a very short space of time in 1863.

Bridges of cast- and wrought-iron spans became quite commonplace in the second half of the 19th century. As well as bridging wide rivers relatively simply, cast iron had the additional advantage of decoration being incorporated into the design at little extra cost. An example of this is Skeldergate Bridge, again in York, opened in 1881, designed also by Thomas Page, this time with his son, George Gordon Page. The three arches have Tudor profiles, the spandrels and parapets are pierced with Gothic quatrefoils, and the stone piers are crenellated. Like many roads and bridges in the

19th century, its cost was recouped by charging tolls to users, and the toll house is an integral part of the design.

The principle of charging tolls to travellers had become well established in the 18th century, with the advent of turnpike roads. An act of parliament was required to enable a turnpike trust to take over a section of highway, along which people had had a right to travel, even if such travel had in practice been almost impossible. The trustees, drawn from local worthies, businessmen and landowners, improved sections of road, and were permitted to charge travellers in proportion to the length of road they had used, and the wear and tear they had exerted upon it. Thus horse-drawn carriages and carts were charged more than hand-carts, and heavy four-footed animals such as horses and oxen were charged more than swine or sheep, or even geese, at that time still commonly driven on foot to market.

101. Ouse Bridge, York, designed by Peter Atkinson, junior.

102. Middleham Bridge, built as a suspension bridge in 1829.

103. Valley Bridge, Scarborough of 1865, re-using the ironwork of
the first Lendal Bridge at York which collapsed during construction.

104.   Lendal Bridge, York, opened in 1863.

105.   Skeldergate Bridge, York, opened in 1881.

The roads were barred at intervals with gates, or 'pikes', laid across them, which were only 'turned', or opened, when the toll had been paid, hence the name. People were at first employed to collect the tolls, although later it became common to farm out, or let, the contract for toll collection, a privilege for which a rent was paid. The toll-collector and his family were housed in small cottages built at the very edge of the road as it then existed, for the gate usually abutted on to it. For this reason, the majority have been demolished, in order either to widen the road or to remove an obstacle to sight-lines. Such toll-houses as do survive seem very small by modern standards, but in their day provided rather better than average accommodation. At Punchard, in upper Arkengarthdale, not far from the *Tan Hill Inn,* a former toll cottage of late 18th-century date has only two rooms. One housed the toll-collector's family, the other served as the office, with its own door and window. Each room has a fireplace, burning coal mined in the remote Tan Hill area, and one of the main commodities of the Reeth and Tan Hill Turnpike Road. Other toll houses are more conspicuous and characterful. Many were single-storey cottages, having a canted bay with windows projecting out into the road, to give the toll-collector good visibility, and to help bar the road, as at Skelton, north of York, on the old line of the A19.

106. Punchard Toll House, Arkengarthdale.

107. Turnpike Toll House of *c.*1800 on old line of the A19 at Skelton, north of York.

Near Faceby, on the A172 between Northallerton and Middlesbrough, a rather grander toll-house survives, with Georgian windows and a Gibbs surround to the front door. Another architectural detail, an ogee hood mould, decorates the lintels of the former toll-house on the A62 near Roberttown, which has a very pronounced canted projection. A rarer survival is the two-storey toll-house at Steanor Bottom, near Todmorden, almost on the Lancashire border. Instead of merely having a canted projection, the whole building is hexagonal in plan, with round-headed windows. The building, dating from the early 19th century, has recently been restored, and the original board, displaying the various toll charges, has been put back in the blank window above the door.

A variation on the turnpike theme was the tontine, a system whereby money, borrowed from individuals to pay for the cost of roadworks, was paid back as annuities. The *Cleveland Tontine Inn,* near Osmotherley, commemorates such a scheme. Impressive stables, with Gothick motifs, were built at the inn in 1806 when the Yarm–Thirsk Turnpike opened for use. One of the primary users was the Sunderland mail coach, which connected with the London coach at Boroughbridge, on the Great North Road about half-way between London and Edinburgh. Its main industry was transport, and there were several coaching inns, but its prosperity suffered badly when the A1 bypass opened in the 1960s, instantly removing a frustrating bottleneck for drivers, but also eliminating its main trade at one fell swoop.

The improvements effected by turnpike trusts made travelling by wheeled transport on main routes much easier from the second half of the 18th century. Regular services were run with stage-coaches, large, relatively comfortable passenger vehicles drawn by teams of horses. The horses were changed at regular stopping places in between stages, and the passengers, too, could obtain comfort and refreshment at the coaching inns, which provided accommodation and extensive stabling. For the first time it became possible to predict—to within a few hours at least—the number of days a journey would take, and so people could arrange to meet at a certain inn in London on, say, Thursday, a facility which benefited industrial enterprises considerably. However, the extensive transportation of raw materials and manufactured goods was more concerned with first canal and then railway development.

It is perhaps appropriate to include here two footnotes to the story of road transport. The first is the provision of seaside piers and promenades, mainly in the second half of the 19th century, when the railways made travelling for pleasure a possibility for the majority of working people. The Halfpenny Bridge at Saltburn was built in 1869 primarily to provide a leisure resource in that seaside town. It was not suitable for heavy traffic, and was used mainly by holiday-makers, before being demolished in 1974. The name came from the toll of one old halfpenny which was charged per person on foot. The change to decimal coinage in 1972 saw the destruction of many ancient toll boards with charges still advertised in the old currency. A larger toll-house, dating from 1906, forms a prominent feature at Scarborough, where it gave access to the Marine Drive, an expensively-built roadway along the seafront, providing visitors with the means of getting sea-air even when the tide was in. The tourists mainly travelled to Scarborough by train on day excursions, and either walked, or took cabs, when there.

108. Toll House at Faceby on the A172.

109. Toll House on the A62 near Roberttown.

110. Steanor Bottom Toll House with surviving toll board.

111. Stables built in 1806 at the Cleveland Tontine Inn near Osmotherley.

112.   Halfpenny Bridge, Saltburn.

113.   Halfpenny Bridge: note the slender columns and elegant ironwork.

114. Halfpenny Bridge: Toll House.

115. Halfpenny Bridge: Toll Board.

116.   Halfpenny Bridge, Saltburn: ticket-collector's
booth and turnstile.

117.   Toll House on the Marine Drive, Scarborough,
1906.

118. Tram-sheds at Bradford, 1915.

119. Tram-sheds at Fulford, near York.

The second footnote concerns the provision of trams as a form of public transport within cities, which required a new form of architecture for their storage. The tram-sheds of 1915 at Bradford are now used for buses, but some of the poles which carried the overhead wires remain. At Fulford, on the outskirts of York, the late 19th-century tram-sheds have been converted to a garage, so in both cases a transport use continues.

Water

From ancient times, men have used rivers and the sea for transport, although there are few structures bearing testimony to that use before relatively modern times. One of the earliest Yorkshire examples is the old lighthouse at Flamborough Head, an octagonal tower of four stages, built of chalk and probably dating from *c.* 1674. Some of the purposes of sea journeys, such as fishing, have survived, albeit in changed form. Others have ceased altogether. The once-intensive whaling industry based on Whitby has left behind few memorials, one of which is the pair of whale-bones to be seen at Sleights. Not only have the purposes of water transport changed, but over the centuries their locations have altered. The old Humberside port of Hedon was extremely important in medieval times, but lost out to Hull as the sea receded, and today the village is well inland, its once bustling harbour and haven merely a boggy depression.

Hull, a relative latecomer to Yorkshire's medieval trade, quickly gained supremacy, and the seaport served as the county's main outlet for trade with the Baltic countries, most of which had already passed through the port of York. Hull saw a particularly early expression of the dramatic change in scale of operation associated with the Industrial Revolution, as witnessed by the impressive Pease Warehouses which are situated in the High Street in the Old Town, but face the river Hull. They were built by Joseph Pease, one of Hull's wealthiest merchants who provided the town's first banking facilities, and led the way in its industrial activities.

The warehouses were built in two phases, in 1745 and 1760, and bear these dates and the initials of Joseph Pease. The structure is of load-bearing brickwork, pierced by regularly-spaced, but relatively small windows under segmental-arched lintels, intended to provide basic daylighting and, above all, ventilation to the interior, with its stout timber framing. By contrast, the Ceres Warehouse added next door in the late 19th century, with a cast-iron framed structure, has much larger windows as its walls are not load-bearing. The pleasing functionalism of the early warehouses makes an interesting comparison with the former Dock Office, which, although built as late as *c.* 1820, is intended to look like an 18th-century town house of the date of the Pease warehouses.

The seaport warehouses retained a utilitarian honesty, the earlier ones limiting the amount of wall structure removed for the provision of windows, and also minimising the spans of roof and floor beams. The structural device of repeating the roof spans many times over a vast warehouse, and thus apparently reducing its bulk into manageable proportions, was used to good effect by dock engineers in many big seaports, as can be seen in the warehouse (*c.* 1850) of Hull Railway Dock, designed in 1846 by the great J. B. Hartley of Liverpool, who came from the West Riding, and served as bridgemaster there.

120. Old lighthouse at Flamborough Head.

121. Whale-bones at Sleights.

122. Hedon Haven.

123. Pease Warehouses, Hull: the earliest section consists of the white arch in the centre and three bays of windows on either side. It is dated *1745* on the imposts of the arch, on the keystone of which are the initials *IP* of Joseph Pease. The section to the left is dated *1760* on the other arch. The Ceres Warehouse on the right was added in the late 19th century.

124.   Georgian elegance of the former Dock Office, Hull, *c.* 1820.

125.   Hull Warehouse No. 6 of *c.*1830. The windows still occupy quite a small percentage of wall area, and the roof spans are restricted. Note the typical 'factory' window frames, which although resembling the proportions of Georgian sash windows, are centrally pivoted.

126.   Warehouse of *c.*1850 at Hull Railway Dock, with a pleasing rhythm of roof gables which reduce the scale of its vast bulk.

Later in the 19th century, an attempt was made to treat the warehouses more decoratively. The structural use of cast-iron frames enabled the panels in between to be thinner, and to contain more windows. The Hull Ships Stores warehouse beside the North Bridge shows this. Here the skyline is emphasised by the use of a decorative terracotta cornice and mansard turrets at the corners, which are reminiscent of French chateaux.

127. Late 19th-century warehouse of Hull Ships Stores. Note the tie-rods, signifying a cast-iron frame inside the building, and thinner panels of brickwork with windows, also the decorative cornice and the corner turrets with mansard roofs.

A few miles north up the river Hull is another attractive building. Near Tickton, alongside the old bridge, which was the only one over the river between Hull and Driffield, is a seed-crushing mill, built not long after the navigation of the river was improved in 1767. The two-storey building, in brick with a deep pantile roof, is surmounted by the remains of a clock tower with pyramidal lead-covered roof, topped by a weather-vane. Four courses of projecting brickwork form a string between the two storeys, and six courses form an overhanging eaves cornice, indicating the 18th-century date. Alongside is a slightly later addition, with side-sliding sash windows. The seeds were imported through Hull and brought upstream to be crushed for their oil, the residue becoming cattle-cake for the farms on the nearby lowlands. Seed-crushing ceased in 1942 and was replaced by fertilizer manufacture.

Considerable efforts were made in the early phases of the Industrial Revolution to improve the navigation of those rivers which had historically been navigable. As with turnpike roads, interference with a waterway required an act of parliament. The first such act concerning a Yorkshire navigation was passed in 1699, and affected the rivers Aire and Calder. Its main intention was to facilitate the import of wool, and the export of cloth, through Hull. This pioneering venture was one of the most successful commercially. Several interesting buildings survive near the terminus behind Dock Street, in Leeds, such as dry docks, and warehouses of various dates, including the late 19th-century building of the Leeds, Goole and Hull Transport Co., Ltd., with deeply over-sailing eaves, an architectural feature often associated with Continental buildings, where the intention is to protect workers from the sun: in Leeds it presumably protected them from the rain.

128. 18th-century seed-crushing mill at Hull Bridge near Tickton.

129.   Terminal of Aire and Calder Navigation Company, Dock Street, Leeds, *c*.1840 (MG).

130.   Warehouses near head of Aire and Calder Navigation, Leeds. The gable furthest to the left is the oldest dating from the late 18th century.

131. Warehouse of the Leeds, Goole and Hull Transport Co. Ltd., in Dock Street, Leeds, with oversailing gables.

132. Main entrance of Banqueting House of the Ouse Navigation Trustees, Naburn in 1973 before subsequent restoration, almost hidden behind overgrown shrubbery. The single-storey banqueting room is on the right, and on the left was the two-storey caretaker's accommodation.

Only shortly after the Aire and Calder Act, another act was passed, in 1702, to make the river Derwent in rural east Yorkshire navigable. This was due in part to the owners of the lands along its banks having industrial interests, notably coal-mining in south Yorkshire, and to the ready market in the growing industrialised areas for the corn grown on the Yorkshire Wolds. One of the main problems faced by the navigation was the construction of cuts around the weirs for corn watermills all along the Derwent, which were themselves there because of both the corn grown on the Wolds, and the water-power provided by the Derwent. Soon they also benefited from the increased trade provided by the Navigation.

The city of York, historically a major port for sea-going vessels (at high tide at least) was loath to see its commercial status undermined by upstart industrial towns, with navigations which could accommodate sea-going craft more comfortably. Under the 1462 Charter of Edward IV, York Corporation had been made conservators of the Ouse and its tributaries. This considerable power had been eroded by the recent navigation acts when in the 18th century strenuous efforts were made to improve the depth of water in the city. An Act of 1727 allowed jetties to be formed to reduce the width of the river, and in 1757 a weir and lock were constructed just below York at Naburn, which raised the draught at York by 1.5m.

133. Side elevation of main dining room of Banqueting House of the Ouse Navigation Trustees, Naburn, in 1973.

However, the gain was temporary, for York's commercial prosperity had long been on an inherently irrevocable decline. The Corporation seems to have reacted to this decadence in a manner not infrequently found under such circumstances: they indulged themselves in an item of architectural folly for which there was really no justification. Alongside Naburn Lock, they built in 1823 a sumptuous Banqueting House at a cost of £2,742, a sum which the then income of the navigation could not easily meet. It was ostensibly to be used for committee meetings of the trustees, although at the time they seem to have met very infrequently. Local feelings against this extravagance ran so high that when in 1833 commissioners visited York to gather information in the preliminaries before the Municipal Corporations Act of 1835, it was cited as an example of the old Corporation's irresponsible squandering of capital. Nevertheless, despite these allegations, and again not unusually in such circumstances, the resulting building is of considerable architectural interest, not least because of its unique nature. After having been a white elephant for more than 150 years, it has recently been restored as a restaurant serving York's enormously-successful tourist industry.

134. Bonding Warehouse beside Skeldergate Bridge, York, 1875.

135. Queen's Staith, York: warehouse converted to office use.

136. Advertisement hoardings decorate derelict warehouses on Queen's Staith, York, no doubt aimed at the passengers in the many bus services which cross the Ouse Bridge.

In York itself there are several old warehouses alongside the river Ouse, although many fine buildings there have been demolished in recent years. In a further attempt to arrest the 19th-century decline of sea-going shipping, it was proposed to provide a bonding warehouse, but this was not constructed until 1875 and never played a major role in the river trade, although it, too, has recently been most successfully converted into a restaurant complex. Nearby, alongside Queen's Staith, some old warehouses have found suitable new users, such as that now the offices of Claxton and Garland, builders and contractors, who made good advertising use of the building's prominent riverside location, and of a traditional style of lettering on a painted band of brickwork previously used to identify the corn merchants who built it. Nearer Ouse Bridge, other warehouses are still derelict, their main function being as a well-established site for the display of hoardings, otherwise frowned on in a heritage-conscious city.

As a result of the improvements to the Ouse, an act was passed in 1793 to make navigable the little tributary river Foss, which joins the Ouse at York. A great many problems were met during construction, not the least of which was a shortage of water. A waterway was eventually opened as far as Sheriff Hutton—short of the original target of Stillington—but was never commercially successful far above York. The navigation was largely abandoned in 1859, leaving most of the locks high and dry. There are few surviving structures, one of which is the New Bridge at Strensall of *c.* 1796, designed by Mr. Scruton, the company's engineer at that time. The bridge is of brick, with a four-centred ashlar stone arch of 'flattened horse-shoe' shape, typical of canal bridges.

137.   New Bridge, Strensall on the Foss Navigation, *c.* 1796.

138. The Canal Basin, Bedale.

Other canal schemes were even less successful. At Bedale there is a canal basin, engagingly referred to locally as the Harbour, which is virtually all that remains of the attempts to make navigable the Bedale Beck from its junction with the river Swale to Bedale. An act for this purpose was passed in 1767, and construction began, but was never completed. The basin is well-built, and still contains the iron rings built into its walls to which it was hoped barges would soon be tied. A weir at the top end of the basin also gave a head of water to the nearby Aiskew corn mill. Alongside the beck, just upstream of the basin, is another historic relic, a small brick building with pointed window openings and castellated parapets, in which leeches were reared for medical purposes.

The year 1767 was a vintage year for Yorkshire canals. Another act was passed which resulted in Ripon becoming the most northerly point of the country's inland waterways system. The river Ure was made navigable from its junction with the Swale, through Boroughbridge, to Ox Close, from whence a 2¼-mile length of canal to Ripon was constructed 1770–73. The canal basin on the outskirts of Ripon survives, with a warehouse built *c.* 1780 of pink sandstone with a hipped pantile roof, again of double-span. The main trade was of coal coming into Ripon, and lead, mined in the Yorkshire Dales, going outward.

139. Leech House alongside Bedale Beck.

140. Warehouses of *c*.1780 at the Canal Basin, Ripon.

The same year—1767—saw yet another act passed, for the Driffield Navigation. Driffield had just been accessible from Hull by boat, but a considerable outlay was necessary to enable Humber keels to reach the town. The navigation opened relatively quickly, in 1770. Several early buildings survive around the canal head, including Mortimer's Warehouse of *c.* 1800. Other East Riding canals linked Market Weighton and Pocklington with the rest of Yorkshire, serving a dual purpose for both navigation and drainage, associated with agricultural improvements. Greater areas of land made suitable for better arable farming increased the products available for transport down the canals to the West Riding.

Pocklington Canal, opened in 1818, had the rare distinction of costing less than anticipated when its act was passed in 1815. At the canal head, just outside Pocklington, is a warehouse, probably the public warehouse built there *c.* 1820 by Thomas Johnson of Pocklington. It has relatively small openings in the brick walls, and segmental-arched lintels, and the pantile roof may have been lifted from a height of two, to three, storeys. Nearby are the ruins of a bone-crushing mill, steam-powered by coal brought along the navigation, which produced fertilizer for the agricultural 'industry' in the area. The canal company built identical bridges along the length of the canal, for example at Thornton, and Walbut Lock, both near Pocklington. They are of brick, each with a four-centred arch of ashlar sandstone voussoirs, and the parapets are curved on plan.

141. Mortimer's Warehouse, Canalhead, Driffield, *c.* 1800.

142. Pocklington Canal Head, with warehouse and ruins of bone-crushing mill.

143. Warehouse at Pocklington Canal Head, *c.*1820 with small openings under segmental-arched lintels.

144. Thornton Bridge on the Pocklington Canal.

145. Bridge at Walbut Lock on the Pocklington Canal.

Huddersfield was the focal point of two canals, which contributed considerably to its sustained growth as a cloth town. The first was built by, and named after, Sir John Ramsden, the lord of the manor. It opened in late 1776, and connected the King's Mill, an ancient fulling mill on the outskirts of Huddersfield, the availability of which was largely responsible for the growth of the town's textile industry, with the Calder and Hebble Navigation at Cooper Bridge, just below the town, 3¾ miles away. It has along this short length a unique turnbridge, dating from 1865, the deck of which could be lifted vertically, parallel with the water, on a series of large wheels and chains suspended from overhead girders.

This canal is often referred to as Huddersfield Broad Canal, to distinguish it from the Huddersfield Narrow Canal, or Huddersfield Canal. This provided the second cross-Pennine waterway, and was opened in 1811, 17 years after its enabling act. The name has arisen because the numerous locks climbing over the watershed were very narrow, necessitating tedious transhipment to the company's own vessels from those of other linking waterways. One of the reasons for the narrow gauge was the route chosen, for this involved the excavation of the famous Stanedge tunnel, at over three miles the longest canal tunnel in the country, and now sadly closed. It was, understandably, formed to the narrowest possible dimensions, with no towpath, the bargees having to work through the tunnel by lying on their backs on top of their barge, and 'legging' against the roof and side of the tunnel for over two hours. The Rochdale Canal, opened in 1804, joining the Calder and Hebble Navigation at Sowerby Bridge, provided a wider and therefore more convenient waterway, but took a longer route to Manchester.

146. Turnbridge on Huddersfield Broad Canal.

147. Leeds and Liverpool Canal Company Warehouse at start of canal in Leeds, *c.*1806 (MG).

148. Five-Rise Staircase of Locks, Bingley, 1774.

The Leeds and Liverpool Canal was the first of the three trans-Pennine waterways to be begun, under an act of 1770, and the last to be completed, in 1816. It is the longest canal, being 127 miles from the river Mersey to its junction with the river Aire in Leeds, from which it connects with Hull along the Aire and Calder Navigation, and it is the only Pennine route still open. At its start in Leeds is a fine stone warehouse dating from *c.* 1806, with Georgian proportions, a rhythmic arrangement of openings, and since it was built early in the 19th century still has internal construction of timber, not cast iron. At Bingley, the famous Five-Rise locks, which lift the canal nearly 20m., over a distance of 100m., provide one of the most spectacular lock staircases ever constructed. It was opened in 1774, and designed by John Longbotham of Halifax, the engineer to the Leeds and Liverpool Canal.

We must return to the Aire and Calder Navigation for the grand finale of Yorkshire's canal story, and to the creation of Goole as a canal town, developed by the navigation company after an act passed in 1820 for a new stretch of canal, which was opened in 1826, from the river Aire at Knottingley, to the then insignificant hamlet of Goole. Little survives of the original company development, but illustrated here is a terrace in Adam Street, dating from *c.* 1830, with a curved street corner typical of the company's buildings. The houses, which appear to be of two storeys, have a basement visible from the rear, due to the land having been levelled up when the development was laid out.

149. Adam Street, Goole: terrace of houses with rounded corner, built *c.* 1830 by the Aire and Calder Navigation Company.

150. Narrow hand-cranked swing bridge, Goole.

The new port of Goole flourished, despite opposition from the Hull docks, and in 1848 the Lancashire and Yorkshire Railway decided to make Goole its eastern port. This collaboration between a canal and a railway operation was highly significant, for most canals were eventually acquired by railway companies and deliberately run down to minimise competition. Goole, however, prospered throughout the 19th century, as its engineering structures testify, such as the hand-cranked, narrow swing bridge on the docks.

A phenomenon peculiar to Goole was the 'Tom Pudding' system, whereby trains of small container-boats of coal were towed by a tug from the Yorkshire coalfield along the navigation to Goole. There a special hoist raised them bodily out of the water, to tip their contents into the holds of ships for export by sea. The hoist was originally powered by the centralised hydraulic system installed in the docks. This unique coal transportation system was installed in the 1860s, having been developed by the Aire and Calder Navigation Company's engineer, W. H. Bartholomew.

151.   Hoist for lifting Tom Puddings.

Railways

The railway system has its origins in the coastal coal-mining areas of Northumberland and Durham, where inclined tramways took wagons, running on wooden tracks, by gravity, down to nearby rivers and the sea. Eventually cast-iron rails were used, and the next step was to apply steam-powered locomotion on rails. In 1758 an act of parliament authorised Charles Brandling, lord of the manor of Middleton, to build a wooden wagonway the few miles from his Middleton Colliery into Leeds, to connect with the Aire and Calder Navigation. In 1812 the wooden track was replaced by rails in order to try out a high-pressure steam locomotive of the type successfully developed by Richard Trevithick, a Cornish engineer. The experiment worked, and the Middleton Railway became the first commercial user of steam locomotion, albeit all 'in house'.

A few years later, the famous Stockton and Darlington Railway followed suit. This was a more ambitious project, 27 miles long, which opened in 1825 and was the first railway with locomotive power to which there was public access for coal haulage. Steam-hauled passenger services were introduced in 1833. In 1834 the Leeds and Selby steam-operated railway provided an additional route for both passengers and goods between the West Riding and the port of Selby, thus rivalling the Aire and Calder Navigation, a foretaste of the cut-throat competition which was to develop between canals and railways.

The third railway line in Yorkshire was the picturesque Whitby and Pickering Railway, opened in 1835 and engineered by the great railway builder, George Stephenson. It did not, however, use steam locomotion, but was horse-drawn. Carriages resembling stage-coaches were drawn by teams of horses, which were perhaps more powerful than the early locomotives, and certainly better suited to the hilly North York Moors. The rails reduced the friction compared with the same carriage on a road. A tunnel, built to serve the horse-drawn line, survives at Grosmont. It is of much smaller section than most railway tunnels, particularly in width as it only carried a single track. The line only went over to steam power in 1847 when the York and North Midland Railway built a new station in Whitby.

The chairman of this company was George Hudson, the 'Railway King', who eventually became M.P. for Whitby, and was largely responsible for the development of that town as a holiday resort. He also built several other lines and stations on the East Coast and on scenic routes through rural Yorkshire, and he almost invented the idea of a day-trip to the seaside as a recreation within the means of families in the industrial towns. George Hudson was a York draper who was lord mayor of York in 1839, at a time when the imminent arrival of the city's railway line from Normanton was eagerly anticipated. He was determined to make York a major railway centre, and this he did, despite the inadequacies of the site chosen for the original station. This terminus was inside the city walls, and it necessitated the construction of an archway through the medieval wall and rampart. Trains had to back out, and as the seaside traffic increased enormously, the congestion became so great that a new station was eventually built. However, several aspects of the design of the Old Station are significant. First, it was commissioned jointly by two railway companies—the York and North Midland and the Great North of England—and some of the county's greatest

152. York's old railway station by G.T. Andrews, 1840.
153. Pickering Station: a typical G.T. Andrews railway station.

railway architecture was built by two companies in collaboration. Secondly, the architect chosen was George Townsend Andrews, a York architect, who went on to design a great many outstandingly elegant railway buildings for George Hudson. Thirdly, the design which Andrews provided, under considerable difficulties, was to influence the design of innumerable stations later, for it consisted of two blocks—one of offices, and the other of refreshment rooms—on opposite sides of the lines, which were to be spanned by a train-shed roof in cast-iron and glass. This caused considerable problems in its construction, more than 10 years before the same technique was used to such good effect by Joseph Paxton for the famous Crystal Palace. Fourthly, when it was decided, in the 1850s, to add a hotel to the station complex, the decision to add it across the ends of the station buildings, thus forming a U-shaped plan, created a precedent, not only for U-plan station termini, but also for a railway hotel as an integral part of a station complex.

154. Pocklington Station, 1847/8, before conversion to a Sports Hall.

155. Pocklington Station: bow window from Station Master's house onto platform.

156. Pocklington Station: rear wall, supporting roof.

157. Pocklington Station: window in rear wall, with cast-iron frame.

Andrews' stations all have certain similarities, although their style varied considerably between Gothic and Classical architecture. All presented an extremely elegant facade to the fare-paying public, who were assured of the social respectability of travelling by railway because of the gentlemanly architecture of the buildings. All have only one visible entrance, in order to ensure the efficient control of passengers past the ticket office. The entrance is usually emphasised by a portico centrally placed in a long single-storey range, with symmetrically-arranged windows on either side of the door, providing daylight to the waiting rooms, ticket, left luggage and porters' offices and so on. Access to all these rooms is only through a row of doors along the platform, and thus only from inside the station, where windows would be less efficient owing to there being less light. A rear wall, having windows with cast-iron frames, for visual relief, across the lines supports the other side of the cast-iron roof. From the Welsh slate roof of the front office range rise several tall chimney-stacks, serving open fires kept constantly burning in the offices, using coal brought cheaply along the railway. At one end there is usually a two-storey house for the station master, who held an important and responsible position, particularly in a small town. He often had a window in his house looking out on to the platform, to give him a view of what was happening in the station.

Most of these details can clearly be seen at Pocklington station, built in 1847–8, which has a classical arcade in stone to the entrance front of the otherwise brick building. It has now been converted to a sports hall. Nearby is a standard Andrews goods station and an engine shed. A short distance away are a pair of keepers' houses alongside a level crossing, to a design repeated at many Andrews stations, and four linesmen's cottages. The station at Market Weighton, of similar date (now demolished) was a particularly long range, built in yellow brick, with a simpler portico than that at Pocklington, sheltering a fine pulvinated frieze with a bay-leaf garland motif above the main doorway. The length and lowness of Market Weighton station was exaggerated by the removal of the train-shed roof, leaving a derelict range of buildings and a rear supporting wall standing in isolation. A typical section of a G. T. Andrews station, also without its roof, can be seen from the level crossing at Pickering.

At Kirkham Abbey, near Malton, a small halt is equipped with an elegant house in superb ashlar stonework. Stone was also used to build Richmond station, designed in an Elizabethan Gothic style to appease the burgesses of Richmond who felt their medieval town should have a complementary railway station, even though it was built on the opposite side of the river. It has an arcaded *porte-cochère,* which allowed carriages to drop passengers at the very door of the station. Here, instead of strict symmetry, the other range of offices has a bay window below a gable projecting from the waiting room. Inside, two spans of a standard Andrews roof are supported on a central arcade of cast-iron Tudor columns and four-centred arches with pierced spandrels. The station was the terminus on a branch line from Darlington, and has, like Pocklington, found a successful new use since its line closed, this time as a garden centre. Both stations were statutorily listed buildings, so their fine roofs were left intact on closure, a factor which seems to have contributed substantially to their conversion, and thus to their survival.

G. T. Andrews' railway commissions came to a sudden end with the fall from financial grace of George Hudson in 1849. A few other companies commissioned fine

158. Pocklington: goods station.

159. Pocklington: engine shed.

160. Pocklington: level crossing keepers' houses.

railway stations, though none of the same variety and in the same quantity as George Hudson. The very fine station at Huddersfield was another example of two railway companies joining forces to produce monumental architecture, in this case the Lancashire and Yorkshire Railway, and the Huddersfield and Manchester Railway and Canal Company—although this building has no parallels in canal architecture. It was designed by another York architect, J. P. Pritchett the Elder, in 1847. It consists of a central two-storey office block, fronted by a magnificent Corinthian portico worthy of a grand Roman temple, flanked by colonnaded single-storey ranges which terminate in small pavilions, each of which bears a medallion commemorating one of the two railway companies responsible.

Railway lines continued to be built for the rest of the 19th century, their buildings of varying quality. The station at Boroughbridge, of 1875, is remarkably uninteresting, while that at Hawes of 1878, on the Midland link between the Wensleydale line and the West Coast route at Hawes Junction, has the rustic charm characteristic of Midland stations. On popular routes, additional platforms were added to the existing stations, particularly along George Hudson's coastal lines. New platforms for the Scarborough line were added to Malton station, and have attractive cast-iron roofs typical of the North Eastern Railway which superseded Hudson's companies.

The masterpiece of this era must be the second and present station at York, designed by the N.E.R's architect, Thomas Prosser, in 1877. It was built around a curve on the existing line just outside the city walls. Somewhat forbidding externally, the curve of the train-shed must surely be one of the most satisfying spaces of all railway architecture. The segmental-arched ribs are supported on robust Corinthian columns.

161. Pocklington: linesmen's cottages.

162. Market Weighton Station, 1847.

163. Market Weighton: station master's house.

164. Kirkham Abbey: railway house.

Almost as splendid a train-shed, although without the curves, was the somewhat earlier Bradford Exchange station, demolished in 1973 for the construction of the new 'Interchange' building which integrates road and rail passengers.

Besides stations, the railways have had a profound effect on the landscape, particularly with viaducts, which generally add to the aesthetic merits of the scenery. Some are architectural fantasies, as at Knaresborough, where the viaduct of 1851 over the river Nidd has a medieval castellated appearance, intended to harmonise with the castle, and others more sober, as at Larpool, near Whitby, where an austere viaduct of 1884, 300m. long, carried the railway at a height of nearly 40m. across the river Esk. One of the most famous viaducts is that at Ribblehead, a lonely spot on the spectacular Settle–Carlisle line opened in 1876, which is at the time of writing the subject of a fierce campaign against closure.

The railways have played a major role in increasing public awareness of industrial history and architecture. The demolition of London's Euston station 'Arch' in 1962 provoked a response which included the founding of the Victorian Society, an amenity and learned society which has courageously fought many conservation battles, on occasion even for industrial buildings. Railway architecture seems to have bridged a cultural gap, bringing polite architecture—and impressive engineering—to the people, and even allowing the public to enter and use such buildings. This general public participation sets railway architecture apart from most other types of industrial building.

165. Richmond Station of 1848, with Gothic *porte-cochère* and 'Elizabethan' bay window.

166. Richmond Station interior, before restoration: note the fine ironwork, with Tudor motifs.

167. Portico of Huddersfield
Station by J.P. Pritchett the
Elder, 1847.

168. Boroughbridge Station.

169. Hawes Station.

170. Malton Station: cast-iron roofs of the Scarborough platform.

171. Platforms 8 and 9, York Station.

172. Bradford Exchange Station, *c.* 1850.

173. Larpool Viaduct, near Whitby, 1884.

IV

FOOD AND DRINK

General Introduction

THE ARCHITECTURE of food and drink processes has a long history. In medieval times, milling at home was outlawed, and instead each manor had a mill in which corn was ground into flour. There was also usually a malt-kiln, sometimes attached to the corn mill, in which barley was made into malt for home brewing. In many manors, the lord also owned a common oven, in which people could bake their bread made from flour ground at the manorial mill. The lord provided these facilities, and received income from them. Most people's houses at that time were small and insubstantial, built of earth, wattle and daub; materials which could be scavenged. Such houses had no chimneys, simply an open hearth in the centre, which might have a hole in the roof to let out the smoke. It was possible to boil food in a pot over such an open fire, but bread needs a warm chamber enclosed from the naked flame.

The corn mill had to be a robust structure to withstand the strains and stresses of the machinery in use, and to function the machinery itself needed to be accurately made: the bakehouse and malt-kiln had to be of fireproof construction. Only the lord of the manor provided buildings of an adequate standard. In practice mill, kiln and oven were usually 'farmed' by a contractor who had to make enough out of his tolls to pay his rent to the lord as well as make a living for himself.

As time went on, the corn mill continued to serve its local community with little change. The manorial malt-kiln expanded, and in many cases grew into a brewery. As home brewing declined, common breweries increased in number. Eventually, some became large-scale concerns, while others closed. The larger breweries were among the pioneers of steam power. In the later 19th century, malting and brewing followed the general industrial trend and became specialist industries: with large maltings clustered near the barley-growing regions, and large breweries congregating in towns with suitable water supplies.

On the other hand, the business of the communal bakehouse declined as houses were more substantially built, with stone or brick chimneys. Larger houses, from late medieval times, often had special brick bread ovens constructed within the main chimney structure. By the late 18th century, virtually every house had its own cooking and baking facilities, due to two industrial developments: the large-scale mining of coal and its transportation, preferably by water because of its bulk, or, failing that, by turnpike road; and the production of cast-iron kitchen ranges, made in small foundries. Many corn mill, malting and brewery buildings still exist, but generally the bakehouse went out of use too long ago for examples to have survived, although their late usage is documented in some places, including Helmsley and Coxwold.

118

Corn Milling

The village corn mill, whether powered by wind or water, has a unique place in our culture. The slowly-turning sails or waterwheel have been portrayed in pencil and paint, in poetry and prose. It was their timeless quality which captured the imagination; mills stood on the same site for centuries, the machinery apparently turning constantly, which seemed to symbolise man's much-sought-after immortality.

Corn mills are a function of economic history. They began as an element of feudal society, and with the rise of capitalism, they were improved by entrepreneurs. Mills also responded to developments in transport and motive power. Eventually, overtaken by centralisation, flour milling became concentrated in certain areas. Many of the small mills left behind continued for a time to grind animal feeds, though this, too, has mainly ceased. A very few mills have been lovingly maintained in working order, as a reminder of a long tradition, and at Crakehall the watermill has been restored and now produces flour after being static for 50 years.

174. Crakehall Mill before restoration. The derelict waterwheel was in the roof-less lean-to building on the right. Leading to it was the mill-pond, completely silted up. On the left is the miller's house.

175. Crakehall Mill: the skeleton of the waterwheel before restoration.

119

176. Brignall Mill: a pair of millstones without wooden furniture. They have become very thin after years of use and dressing. These were used for grinding animal feeds.

177. Aiskew Mill, first floor: millstones encased in a wooden tun, with a hopper mounted above them. On the wall behind the stones hangs a template for dressing the furrows of their grinding surfaces. On the left is the chain of the sack-hoist.

178. Aiskew Mill, ground floor: in the centre the chute down which fell meal ground between the stones on the floor above, into the wooden ark or into a sack. Note the sack barrow. Behind the door on the right is the gearing.

The grinding of corn into flour is performed by a pair of millstones, one placed on top of the other. The lower bed-stone is fixed, and set into the first floor of the mill. The upper runner-stone is powered, either from above in a windmill, or from below in a watermill. Corn is placed in a wooden hopper mounted on top of the stones, and falls through a central hole, or eye, in the runner-stone. It is ground between the two stones, as the runner revolves at speed, by furrows cut into the inner surfaces of the two stones. These are parallel and arranged in sectors, tangentially to the eye of the stone. The stones are worn down by the grinding process, and have frequently to be recut, so the stones become thinner with use. The stones are encased in a wooden tun to contain the flour, which gravitates towards the edge of the stones by centrifugal force, and descends through a small hole cut into the floor beside the edge of the bed-stone, down a chute and into a sack or bin on the floor below—hence the need to raise the stones above ground floor level.

After the grinding stones, the main piece of machinery was the sack-hoist, which saved the miller carrying up the sacks of corn on to the stones floor. In Yorkshire, most corn mills had an internal hoist, but on a few can be seen the external type, sheltered in a timber-boarded cover or lucam, which is such a feature of watermills in other parts of the country, expecially in East Anglia.

179. Lucam at Allerston Mill near Pickering.

Millstones were eventually superseded by rollers—cylinders of chilled iron—which were found to be successful with foreign varieties of wheat, imported from the colonies in the 19th century to meet the increased food demands of a growing industrial society. The first roller-plant in Yorkshire was installed at Tadcaster in 1879, and was seen by Joseph Rank, a miller whose family had windmills in Hull. He was so impressed that he built himself a roller mill in Hull in 1885.

Only the larger watermills had enough power to work a roller plant, such as that at Topcliffe, and another at Boroughbridge, where the old watermill was powered by a weir across the river Ure. The Ure Navigation had to build a cut around this weir; nevertheless the navigation brought not only corn, but coal for a steam engine to supplement the water power. Steam corn mills, compared with watermills, usually were of tall and narrow proportions, as could be seen at the now-demolished Boroughbridge Mill.

Steam-powered mills grew in size until, at the end of the 19th century, they were in effect large factories. Many such mills functioned near navigations, for it was convenient to bring by water wheat shipped through Hull. Wellington Flour Mills at Malton was built alongside the river Derwent, its gables, regularly-spaced windows and pilaster buttresses reminiscent of dock warehouses. At York, the Hull firm of Leetham's built, about 1895, a huge warehouse, with steam-powered hoists, alongside the canalised river Foss to serve a large flour mill there which burnt down in 1931.

The railways created considerable trade for some corn mills in the second half of the 19th century—and after—for a great many horses were needed to take goods to and from railway stations, and those horses needed good food. In Leeds, Crown Point Provender Mill, a four-storey red brick building with Moorish-style triplet windows, even has a horse's head carved on the keystone over the cart entrance.

Manorial mill buildings were a function of vernacular architecture, built in a simple, unselfconscious style, in local materials. In rural areas, old mills of timber-framed construction, with thatched roofs, survived into the 19th century. In York Minster Library there is a small sketch of the mill at Brompton-on-Swale, captioned as being the first etching ever attempted by Julius Ibbetson (who became a well-known Richmond artist) in 1804. It shows a single-storey, timber-framed building, with a loft under the thatched roof. The waterwheel is half in and half out of the building, and a spare millstone is propped up near the wide doors, through which a small cart loaded with sacks of corn could be backed. The mill, which is on the site of a corn watermill recorded in the Domesday Book, was rebuilt after the sketch was made, but the surviving mill building is clearly on the same site, rather distinctively juxtaposed beside the weir.

Monastic watermills were much better-built than their medieval lay counterparts, and usually seem to have been of stone. The almost intact medieval mill of Fountains Abbey survives close to those splendid ruins, and Easby Abbey, near Richmond, has a complete vaulted tail race, some 200m. in length, which carried water from the mill wheel to flush the canons' reredorter in the abbey complex itself.

Near the ruins of Rievaulx Abbey stands a mill, probably on medieval foundations, which was built in 1706, with a storey added for storage purposes in the late 19th century, when the manorial soke system had given way to merchant milling, and mills needed to hold stocks of grain. The later stonework is of inferior quality to the

180.   Boroughbridge Mill: an ancient watermill, powered by a weir across the river Ure, was supplemented by steam power. The steam mill is tall and narrow. The building on the right is a warehouse into which corn, brought by water, was unloaded by the hoist in the lucam.

181.   Former roller mill in Easingwold, with the stump of the steam engine chimney on the left. Note the 'factory' windows with cast-iron frames, using small, cheap sizes of glass, and having a small pivoting central section which opened for ventilation.

182. Wellington Flour Mills, Malton.

183. Leetham's Warehouse, York, alongside the river Foss.

184. Crown Point Provender Mill, Leeds.

185. Crown Point Provender Mill: detail of goods entrance with horse's head projecting from the keystone.

earlier work, but the carefully-shaped gable coping stones were obviously removed from their original position and re-used at the new level. The 1706 mill already had an internal waterwheel, the access to which was by a door in the gable-end wall, and the wheelchamber was lighted by a window. Just above ground level, another window lit the gearing, and a third ground-floor window served the general working space just inside the round-headed door, which must have served as the miller's office, for on the sill of this window was fixed a wooden desk. Work at the millstones was daylighted by the first-floor window.

On some estates, the concept of the medieval milling monopoly was perpetuated into the 19th century, sometimes with the mill bearing the lord of the manor's coat of arms, or of a lady of the manor, as at West Ayton Mill, near the source of the river Derwent, not far from Scarborough, which bears a carving of the arms of Lady Hewley. The mill, a well-proportioned building, was called Derwent Flour Mills.

186. Brompton-on-Swale Mill in 1804 (*York Minster Library*).

187. The medieval vaulted tail race at Easby Abbey Mill.

188. Rievaulx Mill of 1706, raised in the late 19th century.

189. Derwent Flour Mills, West Ayton, with Lady Hewley's coat of arms.

A few owners recognised the romantic associations of watermills, and transformed their corn mill into an architectural extravaganza. At Howsham, also on the river Derwent, the mill had a dual purpose, and doubled as a folly in the landscape surrounding Howsham Hall. The mill was built about 1755, probably to a design by John Carr, had a pyramidal hipped roof, and its window and door were of Gothick shape. In addition, the facades were decorated with a symmetrical arrangement of blank Gothick windows and quatrefoils, plastered and painted to look as if they had glazing bars. Sadly, this fine building is now in ruins after being destroyed by fire. Not far away from Howsham, another 18th-century mill at Buttercrambe, again on the Derwent, was also give a far from utilitarian appearance. Built in brick, it has projecting quoins, a decorative brickwork motif also repeated around the window and door openings, and in the gable is a keyed oculus feature. All the mills on the lower reaches of the Derwent benefited from the navigation facilities of the river. Two very large mills were built in the 18th century at Sutton-on-Derwent and Stamford Bridge, the former rebuilt on an even larger scale after a fire in 1826, the latter extended at about the same time. Sutton-on-Derwent Mill is now tragically derelict, but Stamford Bridge Mill has been converted into a bar and restaurant complex, complete with turning waterwheel.

Many corn mills are carved with the names of their proud owners, and with dates, which usually commemorate a rebuilding, all in recognition not only of a mill's economic importance, but also of the long history of its site and, as seemed inevitable at the time, its long continuance. At Rosedale Abbey, the lintel over the main doorway into the mill bears the inscription 'George Wilson 1853', and at High Costa Mill, near Pickering, a lintel carries a shield inscribed '1809 IS', referring to the Simpson family who owned it, while at Bransdale, near Helmsley, a mill built of beautiful ashlar stonework has the letters 'W S' on the ends of the tie-rods supporting the loft floor, and the inscription 'Rebuilt 1842' on the lintel of a first-floor window. Matching doorways in the front elevation gave access to the mill and the wheelhouse. The initials are those of William Strickland, the miller, whose son Emanuel, curate of Ingleby Greenhow, had carved on the mill house an inscription of biblical texts in Greek, Hebrew and Latin!

Many village corn mills closed in the late 19th century, as imported wheat ground in large roller mills and transported by railway took their trade, and replaced stone-ground wholemeal flour with refined white flour. More mills ceased working in the 20th century. In the early 1970s, one of the few working waterwheels in Yorkshire was at Sinnington Grange Mill, near Pickering, on the river Seven, where it powered a sack-hoist to lift grain into the mill for drying purposes. The mill has a cast-iron frame, expressed on the outside as a series of tie-rods, and regularly-spaced windows in its brick walls, one of which is blank and carries an inscription panel with the name 'Burton' and the date 1844 in Latin numerals.

Since then, there has been something of a revival of interest in 'health foods', in alternative technology for power sources, and above all in the heritage. York's watermill at its Castle Museum has been joined by that at Worsborough, near Barnsley, the High Corn Mill Industrial and Folk Museum at Skipton, Bainbridge Low Mill, and by Crakehall Mill, already mentioned. Other mills and wheels in the process of restoration include High Costa Mill, and Tocketts Mill, near Guisborough.

190. Sketch of Howsham Mill, *c.*1965.

191. Buttercrambe Mill, with decorative brickwork details.

192. Stamford Bridge Mill, now a bar and restaurant complex.

193. Rosedale Abbey Mill: doorway.

194. High Costa Mill: lintel.

195. Bransdale Mill, rebuilt 1842.

196. Sinnington Grange Mill, 1844.

197. Leatt's Mill, Skipton (MG).

198. Leatt's Mill, Skipton: rear view with Leeds and Liverpool Canal on the left, and mill dam on the right (MG).

Malting and Brewing

The raw materials of ale are pure water and malted barley. The addition of hops produces beer. In medieval times, brewing was a domestic craft which took place in the kitchen, and was performed by the females of the household, the necessary boiling of the water resulting in a safer drink than was otherwise available. In monastic communities, the ale was usually particularly good, a reflection, no doubt, of higher standards of learning, and a more scientific approach to the subject. After the dissolution of the monasteries, Yorkshire, being well endowed with religious houses, was presumably well-off for skilled brewers.

In the puritanical Commonwealth of 1649-60 there was official disapproval of intemperance, and coffee and chocolate became popular products, with tea becoming a fashionable drink shortly afterwards. After the Restoration, beer became acceptable again, and victuallers were licensed by local magistrates to brew and sell their own beer. In the 18th century, some of the more talented brewers, particularly those with supplies of suitable water, began supplying a few outlets other than their own, and so were known as 'common brewers'.

199. Rhodes Brewery, Thirsk: a common brewery of 1803.

200. John Smith's Brewery, Tadcaster.

A rare example of a small common brewery survives at Thirsk. Rhodes Brewery in Kirkgate is situated behind the former pub, originally its sole outlet. In between is the Georgian brewer's house, built on when an expanding business had generated more prosperity. The three-storey brewhouse bears the date 1803, and retains a small chimney which served the steam boiler. Beyond are single-storey buildings which provided stables, barrel-stores, coopering shops and malt stores. At the end of the 19th century, the brewery was taken over by John Smith's Brewery of Tadcaster, and became a bottling and distribution depot. It made economic sense to wash and refill bulky bottles on a regional basis, and only to transport the beer itself from Tadcaster.

In the south of England, a heavily-hopped drink, known as porter, made from soft water, became popular. In the north, the palate preferred a pale ale, using hard water and high quality malt. After the Industrial Revolution, the availability of transport for such bulky goods as malt and beer transformed what had been a community product into a full-scale commercialised industry, located in relatively few specialised centres, such as Malton, and Tadcaster, which still has three functioning breweries dominating the town. In the centre, is John Smith's, built *c.* 1880, actually after the death of John Smith himself. It is on a monumental scale, its large stone building having the variety of forms which invariably create interesting brewery architecture. The site is overshadowed by a large chimney of textured surface, with a corbelled summit, which provides counterpoint to the other buildings. A short distance away stood Hammond's Tower Brewery. Its name commemorated a type of brewing process developed in the 1860s, in which each of the successive stages of beer-production took place on a different level, resulting in a tall brewhouse with a small floor area on several floors, hence the term. By pumping water to the top, relatively cheaply by steam power, the liquor passed down through the various stages by gravity. The Tower Brewery was built in the 1880s, alongside the railway line running into Tadcaster. The now-demolished brewhouse had castellated parapets, and two turret-like chimneys gave it something of the appearance of a medieval castle keep. Another interesting skyline can be seen at East Cowick, near Goole, where the former Hartley's Brewery had buildings clustering around the brewing tower, giving a composition reminiscent of a fairy-tale romantic castle, an effect emphasised by crocketted ridge tiles and a projecting lucam.

The nature of the water used, the degree to which the malt has been cured, and the length of brewing time determine the taste of the beer. Heating water and malt together is known as mashing, and produces wort, which is then boiled, and next fermented. In Yorkshire, fermentation took place in stone cisterns called 'Yorkshire stone squares', the first use of which is attributed to Timothy Bentley of Lockwood Brewery, near Huddersfield, in the late 18th century. Bentley was friendly with Joseph Priestley, a Leeds Unitarian minister who conducted scientific experiments on the mysteries of brewing.

Malting is an accelerated version of what happens when barley corn is sown. The seed contains a supply of starch which feeds the young shoot until its roots make it self-sufficient. The maltster gets the barley to this stage of growth so that the brewer can utilise the sugars in the starch, which will ferment if he adds yeast. To make malt, the barley is first soaked in water, then spread out on the malting floor in a thick layer known as the couch. As the barley sprouts, it is carefully turned with a wooden malt shovel, so favoured as an inn sign, to prevent bruising and thus infection of the corns. After several days of flooring, the green malt is transferred to the kiln and gently dried, both to kill off any further growth, and also to cure it and produce its flavour. Couching floors need to be very strong to bear the weight of a thick layer of barley wet from the cistern. At first the floors were entirely of timber, but in the 19th century, cast-iron columns were used to support the beams carrying the floors, which were often surfaced with perforated earthenware tiles to allow warm air to rise up through the couch. A number of window openings were required, not only to let in light, but to allow the maltster to control ventilation of the building.

The kiln is normally a taller building, with a furnace room on the ground floor below the drying room through which warm air is drawn up by a flue. Fryer's Crown Brewery, a very small firm at Brompton-on-Swale, continued malting and brewing by hand in the old-fashioned way until *c.* 1958. The maltings building still contains the furnace for the kiln where its own barley was malted.

201. Hartley's Brewery, East Cowick.

202. Hammond's Tower Brewery, Tadcaster, now demolished. The old name was painted on the black patch on the brickwork. The replacement modern brewery is seen under construction, to the left.

203. Malt-kiln furnace, Fryer's Crown Brewery,
Brompton-on-Swale.

204. Old maltings, Langthorpe.

205. Later maltings, Langthorpe.

At Langthorpe, near Boroughbridge, is the county's oldest maltings, dating from about 1850. The three-storey brick building contains cast-iron columns, signed 'C. Corcoran 31 Mark Lane', which were probably made in Leeds. At one end is a two-storey kiln, square on plan, with a flue in the form of a brick cone, resembling an oast-house, now minus the cowl which controlled its draught. Close by, near the railway line which brought the barley, is a larger maltings, more typical of most Yorkshire malting buildings. It has a much wider floor area, and at one end a pair of kilns, each with a slate pyramidal roof and an elevated flat-topped flue. Both maltings served Warwick and Co.'s Anchor Brewery, rebuilt in 1856.

Many large maltings were built in the barley-growing regions of the Yorkshire Wolds. One of the first was at Nafferton, built in 1840 as a water-powered combined corn mill and maltings, using the Driffield Navigation for bulk transport. Later, Nafferton concentrated solely on malting, but the waterwheel was retained to power the removal of husks from the barley, and the sack-hoist.

206. Market Weighton Maltings.

Later maltings in this area huddled near the railway lines. At Market Weighton, a 19th-century maltings and brewery was bought in 1901 by John Smith's Brewery, who closed down the brewing side in order to promote their own product, but retained the maltings, rebuilding the kilns in 1915, in order to supply the Tadcaster brewery by rail. It finally closed in 1960, and was converted to an animal feeds mill. The building has a regular pattern of shuttered windows, and the ends of the tie-rods dotted over the walls indicate the cast-iron strengthening of the floors. At one end are the kiln roofs which give such a pleasing silhouette to maltings buildings.

Some firms built maltings and warehouses literally alongside a railway line, as at Skerne Road, where a powerful three-storey building, now used by a large Driffield mill for storage, has a distinctive rhythm of pilaster buttresses, and the centres of its two main facades are dominated by tall projecting lucams, each under a gabled roof, and with a decorative cast-iron guard-rail. In recent years, nearly all traditional maltings have closed, victims of the very centralisation and specialisation which caused them to be built a century or so ago, as they have been superseded by very large malt plants.

207. Nafferton Maltings.

208. Skerne Road Store, Driffield.

V

TEXTILES

Man's need to clothe himself has taken up a great deal of his time throughout history. The transformation of raw wool, greasy and dirty from the sheep's back, into cloth which can be made up into a serviceable yet pleasing garment, involves very many stages. Sheep in the Yorkshire Dales are still sometimes shorn by hand, using shears almost identical to those known to have been in use in Roman times. The contribution made by wool to the nation's economy in medieval times is indicated by the official seat of the Lord Chancellor, the Woolsack.

Making raw wool into cloth for the family's use was a domestic craft carried out in many homes throughout the country. In addition, quality cloths were produced by skilled craftsmen under the jealous control of medieval guilds in towns and cities such as Beverley and York. Through restrictive practices, the cloth industry in those ancient boroughs declined, and areas in the West Riding, outside the guild system, prospered at their expense. Here were ample supplies of soft water suitable for cleansing the wool and the finished cloth: here, too, were streams in hill locations suitable for water-powered mills.

As well as the West Riding cloth industry, in the Yorkshire Dales a substantial knitting industry grew up, also outside the guild system. Stockings and caps were hand-knitted in great quantities in remote cottages, as people walked long distances, particularly to work in the lead mines. The products were sold in this country, and were also exported to the Low Countries, by hosiers, merchants who bought wholesale quantities of wool, had it spun to their specification, and put it out separately to be knitted up. Although the knitting industry never did become mechanised, this kind of capitalised organisation is an important step on the road towards industrialisation.

209. Sheep shearing in the Yorkshire Dales: the man on the left is using powered clippers; the older man on the right prefers hand shears of the type in use since Roman times.

In time, the manufacture of cloth in West Riding cottages became a specialised, albeit hand-powered industry, and the vernacular architecture of the area reflects the particular requirements which this generated for extra light on the first floor, where the loom was kept. Weaving is a skilled occupation, and the saleable quality of the finished product depended upon it, so this task was usually reserved for the male head of the household, while any unmarried women of the family strove to supply him with spun yarn—hence the term 'spinster'. The earlier stages of preparing the wool for spinning, which were messier, were carried out by the wife and children in amongst the general clutter of everyday life.

In the cloth-producing areas of the West Riding, all the cottages had weavers' windows on the first floor. It was not possible to achieve large areas of continuous window, so a lot of small windows were ranged together, often occupying the full length of the house. Obviously, it was difficult for a whole family to devote itself entirely to keeping pace with the bread-winner weaver, so there was a certain amount of specialisation, with some people concentrating on, say, spinning, particularly as this came to be carried out in factories. Weaving families also sometimes pooled resources, building on an extra floor running above several of their houses as a communal weaving chamber.

The cloth was produced in humble cottages by yeoman weavers with little in the way of financial resources, who probably were also engaged in some subsistence agriculture. To sell their piece of cloth, they had to transport it to a recognised cloth market. They might own a pack animal, but were extremely unlikely to own a cart, and many must have had to carry their cloth on their backs. A piece of cloth therefore needed to be the maximum size, by weight, that the weaver could carry, and was not a fixed length: the standard piece in an area which produced coarse cloth was therefore shorter than a piece of finer cloth. The width was about a metre, and related to a convenient distance for the weaver to pass his shuttle from one hand to the other.

At the cloth market, the piece of cloth would, if all went well, be sold to a cloth merchant, a much more prosperous gentleman, a fact inevitably reflected in his architecture. The merchants built themselves cloth halls in which to operate in greater comfort. The first, dating from the 17th century, was at Heptonstall, an old hill-top settlement dedicated to hand-powered cloth production, but which was in the 18th century superseded by younger places down in the valleys, such as Leeds or Halifax, with better communications than pack-horse tracks, and also water power.

The growing towns of the 18th century vied with one another in the building of impressive cloth halls. The merchants were, it can be seen with the benefit of hindsight, building monuments to an era already past its prime, and their grand architecture had but a short-lived future. Only a fragment survives of the Leeds White Cloth Hall of 1775, its distinguished entrance, surmounted by a cupola which contained a clock and bell to indicate the permitted hours of trading, now sadly derelict, most of the hall itself having been cut through by a railway line.

The Piece Hall at Halifax, dating from 1779, is the only complete 18th-century cloth market building in Yorkshire. It has survived because after it ceased to be used for its original purpose, in the 19th century, it became a wholesale fruit and vegetable market, a use which necessitated few physical changes to its splendid structure. In

141

210. 18th-century weaver's cottage near Almondbury: note the use of small panes of glass.

211. Almondbury: early 19th-century weavers' cottages, with one weaving chamber running over two cottages.

212. Almondbury: 19th-century cottages, with weavers' windows continuing as a vernacular architecture motif after the introduction of powered weaving.

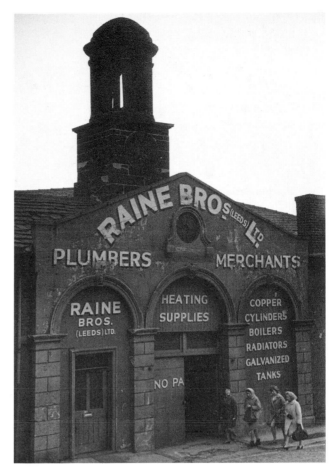

213. White Cloth Hall, Leeds (MG).

214. Main entrance to the Piece Hall, Halifax, before restoration.

1928 it was scheduled as a somewhat unusual Ancient Monument, fortuitous recognition which saved it from subsequent demolition, and more recently it has been well restored, and sensitively converted into Halifax's main tourist attraction, with a museum, information office, exhibition space, craft shops and cafe. If not as ancient as Roman forts and medieval castles, the building is certainly monumental. It consists of a great open quadrangle, in which once stood the cottage-dwellers with their cloth. On all four sides are ordered rows of small offices, which were occupied by the prosperous cloth merchants. The outer walls are blank, except for the majestic gateways, for such was the value of cloth that the building was designed introspectively, with security in mind. The three hundred-plus members' rooms all face inwards on to the quadrangle, and the colonnaded access galleries on each floor contain a door and a sash window to every room.

215. Birk's Mill, Almondbury: front elevation.

Until the middle of the 18th century, the only mechanised process in the manufacture of woollen cloth was fulling, and that had been mechanised since the Middle Ages. Heavy wooden hammers, lifted up by a ratchet operated by a waterwheel, dropped on to the cloth, pounding it in a tub of water and chemicals. This shrank the cloth, and 'milled it up', fusing it into a much stronger fabric than that which came off the loom. It then had to be dried, and stretched back into an orderly shape, a process achieved on tenters, large open-air clothes-horses equipped with small sharp hooks on to which the cloth was hung, first from the top. The bottom bar was loose, and was attached to the other selvage side of the cloth, then eased into place, a task which it was tempting to do with one's body weight, in a sitting position—though if doing so, one was likely to jump suddenly—on, or off, the tenterhooks! Fulling mills were small, insignificant buildings, located at suitable water-powered sites within reasonable distance of weaving communities, such as Birk's Mill, near Almondbury, a plain building surrounded by weavers' cottages.

144

In 1733, John Kay of Bury invented the 'flying shuttle', which allowed a weaver to weave a wider piece of cloth than his own convenient reach, and at a faster pace. The trouble was, the hand-spinners could not keep up with him. Several inventors turned their attention to the mechanisation of spinning, notably James Hargreaves, who produced the hand-powered spinning-jenny in 1764, Richard Arkwright, who developed the water-frame in 1769, and Samuel Crompton, whose spinning-mule of 1780 was originally hand-powered.

These machines were first developed for cotton spinning, a new problem which demanded new approaches, whereas many people were set in their ways in woollen manufacture. Nevertheless, the machines were eventually adapted for wool, but the mechanisation of the industry was a very gradual process, weaving in particular continuing as a hand craft. Perhaps more than any other, industrialisation of the textile industry was a process of evolution rather than revolution.

216. Birk's Mill, Almondbury: rear elevation.

Small mills were built to do a particular stage as a machine became available, often a relatively simple preparatory process, such as 'scribbling'—opening up the jumbled fibres and straightening them out before spinning. Many of these early mills were built in seemingly unlikely places, such as Hawes, which has been mentioned already. Another such site was Boynton, near Bridlington, where a water-powered woollen manufactory was built c. 1770 to give employment on a country estate. The building, in brick with a pantile roof, is of classical proportions, and symmetrical in composition, with blank circular details, betraying its gentlemanly origins.

The economic background of woollen manufacture, in the hands of a large number of independent, small-scale owners who, one suspects, adapted to the new system with some reluctance, resulted in a fairly low up-take of industrialisation, and little architecture of merit. Small fulling mills fulled, small scribbling mills scribbled, both serving otherwise hand-powered workers, and later small spinning mills spun. There was little integration. A rare exception was a textile complex at Sowerby Bridge, an industrial settlement which grew up in the late 18th and early 19th centuries around an old fulling mill beside a bridge over the river Calder. The fulling mill was joined, in the second half of the 18th century, by a scribbling mill, and a large hand-loom

217. Woollen Manufactory, Boynton near Bridlington: a classical composition of *c.*1770.

218. John Brooke and Sons, Armitage Bridge, Huddersfield: one of the largest woollen mills in the area (MG).

workshop was built alongside the old road leading to the bridge. The loomshop was, unusually, in such a predominantly stone-built area, of brick, perhaps an indication of its prestige as a local milestone of textile development, at a time when the most fashionable Georgian buildings were of brick. It has five storeys of three-light mullioned windows. A narrow building, it originally had these windows to both front and back, and inside were arranged two rows of small hand-looms, one beside each window, for the weavers to receive good daylight. Later, the turnpike road passed behind the loomshop at a much higher level, blocking out its light, but by then a new steam-powered spinning mill had been added to the site, and the use of hand-looms was declining.

At the very end of the 18th century, a young, well-to-do Leeds merchant, called Benjamin Gott, built a fully integrated woollen mill much larger than others in existence at the time, partly because he had the money for a large one. Bean Ing Mill was well-equipped in 1793, with one of the first Boulton and Watt steam engines to be installed in a textile mill, yet at the time there were few powered machines available. In the 19th century larger woollen mills became more common, although rarely as large as most worsted mills. Though an important historical precursor, Bean Ing Mill was demolished in the 1960s; however, a mill at Armley rebuilt by Gott in 1805 has been turned into an industrial museum specialising in textile history. John Brooke and Sons of Armitage Bridge, established in 1819, was one of the largest woollen mills in the Huddersfield area. Originally water-powered, and with weavers' cottages close by in the Holme Valley, it gradually mechanised all processes, and c. 1870 translated its integration into the worsted side of the textile industry.

219. Joseph Sykes' Mill, Brockholes: a unique example of a mill for both woollen and worsted manufacture (MG).

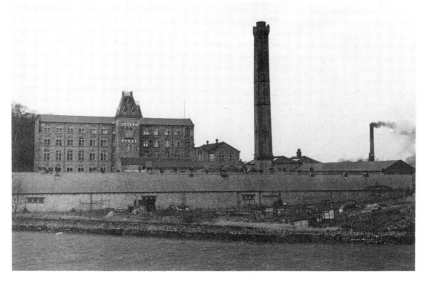

The worsted industry, producing a higher quality finished product, mechanised earlier. The manufacture of worsted cloth in Yorkshire increased in the 18th century, partly because the longer worsted fibres were closer in character to those of cotton than was shorter staple wool, thus cotton machines were easier to adapt to a worsted than a woollen application. Like cotton, the newer industry was more amenable to new ways, and it had a larger-scale capital funding. This allowed larger—and grander—buildings to emerge from the worsted sector. Joseph Sykes' Mill at Brockholes, near Huddersfield, built in 1880, was the only mill in Europe designed to process raw Australian wool into both woollen and worsted cloths.

The relatively early mechanisation of worsted spinning meant that many of even the large mills were originally water-powered. At Goose Eye, near Keighley, a water-powered worsted spinning mill was built as late as the mid-1840s, and another mill of similar date in the same area, Providence Mills at Wilsden, was surrounded by cottages with hand-powered workers living alongside. Nearer Bradford, steam power was adopted much earlier. John Foster and Sons' Black Dyke Mills was established as an upland steam-powered worsted mill from 1835 due to the availability of coal at Queensbury. Later mills were able to take advantage of better transport facilities, such as Bairstow's Mill, Sutton in Craven, alongside the Leeds and Liverpool Canal. When Sir Titus Salt established the famous Saltaire settlement around his huge new integrated mill in 1850, he had the benefit of the river Aire for water for washing his wool, the Leeds and Liverpool Canal and the railway for transport.

At the other end of the market from worsted was the manufacture of cloth from 'mungo' and 'shoddy'—yarns made from recycled rags. These trades were centred on Batley and Dewsbury, and the rag merchants there seem to have tried hard to compensate for the slightly 'non-U' image of their business by investing in particularly fine buildings. Cloth Hall Mills in Foundry Street, Dewsbury, of 1874, has medallions of Victorian figures such as Disraeli and Gladstone on its classical street facade. At Batley, warehouses near the railway station form a most imposing group, with a double-curved facade, having a convex corner, and concave wall beyond, with cusped arches of Moorish shape, and an elegant projecting cornice.

These warehouses were intended to give a respectable image to potential customers arriving by train, and were sited so as to cause them to travel as little additional distance as possible. Warehouses with a similar intention, but for high-quality worsted cloths, can be seen in a whole area of Bradford, in between the former Exchange and Forster Square stations. The area is known as 'Little Germany', because a great many German merchants settled in Bradford in the 19th century. They imported Continental wool, which was made into good cloth in Bradford, and then often exported back to Germany, particularly for military use. Customers visited the Little Germany warehouses-cum-offices, and so needed to be reassured of the merchants' respectability by their impressive architecture. The architectural appearance of the warehouses was based on Italian *palazzi,* and they were designed by leading Bradford architects of the day.

An equally astonishing warehouse in Park Square, Leeds, was built for Sir John Barran, the pioneer of ready-made clothing, in 1878. It was designed by Leeds architect Thomas Ambler, with an elaborate eclectic use of Moorish architectural details, in brick, with terracotta decoration. It has recently been converted to office

220. Turkey Mills, Goose Eye: general view (MG).

221. Turkey Mills, Goose Eye: original
water-powered mill on right (MG).

222. Turkey Mills, Goose Eye: spinning mill with paper mill dam in foreground (MG).

223. Black Dyke Mills, Queensbury (MG).

224. Black Dyke Mills: impressive entrance expressing status of the quality product (MG).

225. T & M Bairstow Ltd: Sutton in Craven, 1888 (MG).

226. Cloth Hall Mills, Dewsbury (MG).

227. Warehouse near Batley Station (MG).

228. Sowerby Bridge: steam-powered spinning mill on the right.

229. Little Germany, Bradford: doorway (MG).

CHURCH BANK STORAGE

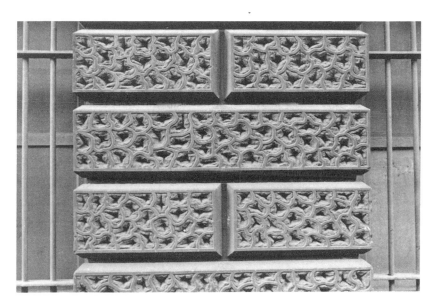

230. Little Germany, Bradford: grill in doorway (MG).

231. Little Germany: fine stonework with vermiculated surface (MG).

232. St Paul's House, Leeds (MG).

233. St Paul's House, Leeds (MG).

234. St Paul's House: details (MG).

235. St Paul's House: terracotta decoration (MG).

accommodation, and the minarets and cresting along the parapets, which had previously been removed, have been successfully replaced by glass-fibre replicas.

Besides woollen and worsted cloths, it was necessary to produce fabrics for household use. Shops still have 'linen' departments because before the importation of cotton, or its substitution by artificial fibres, sheets, towels and underwear were mainly made of linen. Linen cloth is produced from flax, a plant with slender stalks. These were retted to dissolve the sap holding together the stem fibres, which could, after treatment, be spun into yarn, but they were brittle, and difficult to spin by machines. In the early 19th century, a linen industry developed in certain areas, such as Nidderdale, Northallerton and Barnsley. Soon they were joined by Leeds.

A young Leeds linen draper, John Marshall, a man of drive, energy, and a considerable capacity for hard work, was envious of the fortunes being made from cotton spinning over on the other side of the Pennines. In 1787, when he was only 22, his father died, leaving him a small amount of capital. Only days later, he leased a newly-erected water-powered mill on the outskirts of Leeds, and bought some recently-patented flax spinning machines. After much trial and error, and modification of the machines, he made some slight progress, and in 1791 decided to move into Leeds, where there were many male hand-loom linen weavers whose womenfolk would provide a pool of potential factory spinners.

He chose a site in Holbeck, near the head of the Leeds and Liverpool Canal, then in course of construction, along which he correctly envisaged Irish flax being imported before long. Initially, his mill was water-powered, but as steam engines were improved to give a smoother motion, he followed Gott's example and installed a Boulton and Watt engine.

The business prospered, and in 1806 he invested in the building of a warehouse of fireproof construction, with cast-iron columns and beams, instead of timber. In this he was able safely to store quantities of Baltic flax whenever they could be brought along the Aire and Calder Navigation, during the difficult period of the Napoleonic wars. His firm could continue working, while his rivals were often held up due to the sporadic interruption of flax supplies. This taught John Marshall the value of investing in good quality buildings, using the most up-to-date technology.

236. The Office Block, Temple Mills, Marshall Street, Holbeck, Leeds.

His next step was to construct a gas plant so as to be able to light his mill artificially if trade demanded shift working.

In 1816 his son, another John Marshall, entered the business, and the firm built another new mill, this time a six-storey fireproof-construction building powered by a 70 h.p. steam engine, one of the largest of its time. Soon afterwards, the father immersed himself in Whig politics and his own brand of philanthropy, supporting educational establishments, and the Leeds General Infirmary, and establishing a friendly society to cover his male mill-workers in cases of sickness or death. He opened a school in the mill, limiting the working day of child employees so that they could spend some time in the school. This principle was embodied in the 1836 Factory Act, whereby children under 13 spent only half of each day at school. More new buildings followed as it became possible to machine-spin finer linen yarn, and to weave it by machine. Late in the 1830s, John Marshall senior was getting old. His son John had died young in 1836. The third son, James, was head of the firm, and he decided to expand again. This time, the new building was not a multi-storey mill building, but was designed on entirely new lines.

The new mill consisted of a vast, single-storey building, 125m. by 70m., on a cast-iron frame, with a flat roof carried on brick vaulting. Skylights in the roof would provide even daylight into the whole area, and ventilators in the top of each would help to control the internal environment, elaborately warmed, humidified, drained, and powered. This remarkable concept, invented by a man called David Roberts, was implemented by a Leeds engineer, James Combe. The appearance of the building was left in the hands of a Durham architect, Joseph Bonomi the younger, who had spent eight years in Egypt studying ancient architecture there, and was the acknowledged expert on the temples at Karnak, Edfu and Philae. The resulting mill is extraordinary, for its technologically advanced structure is decorated with Egyptian motifs. The cast-iron columns have palm capitals, and outside, the millstone grit ashlar walls contain large cast-iron window-frames interspersed by half-columns with papyrus capitals.

In 1840, James Marshall added an office block, the family always having set great store by administration, accounting and the meticulous keeping of individual work records. Here Bonomi was able to lavish more detailed antiquarian knowledge, for the furniture was of Egyptian design, and the building had a screen facade carefully copied from the portico of the Temple of Horus at Edfu. The Egyptian Revival is one of the less common of the numerous 19th-century revivals of earlier styles of architecture. One can only speculate on the reasons why it so appealed to the Marshalls. The mill certainly became a legend in its own lifetime, making a fictional appearance in the novel *Sybil* written by Benjamin Disraeli, and becoming famous as the mill where sheep grazed on the flat roof. This unlikely-sounding phenomenon is almost certainly fact, not fiction, for documentary evidence shows that the brick vaults were covered on the outside by rough plaster, then by a mixture of coal-tar and lime to form an impervious moisture barrier, rainwater being drained away down the insides of the hollow cast-iron columns. To insulate the delicate waterproof membrane, it was covered over with a 200mm. thick layer of earth, which was sown with grass to hold it in place. The use of sheep to keep the grass short is thus not such a far-fetched part of the story.

237. Temple Mills, Leeds: details (MG).

238. Temple Mills.

Popularly memorable though the sheep may have been, the real significance of the mill is as a remarkably early precursor of 20th-century single-storey factory design. Like so many examples of monumental industrial architecture, Marshall's Mill celebrated the epitome of the firm's success, which had already peaked, and a long, slow decline of the linen industry followed. The building's vast internal space is now used by a mail order company, in itself part of the late 20th-century commercial success story.

VI

MINERAL EXTRACTION

The industries of mineral extraction have, broadly speaking, produced fewer buildings of architectural interest than most other industries. Coal, for example, which is popularly identified with Yorkshire, has associated with it no buildings comparable with the majestic textile mills. Caphouse Colliery, at Overton, near Wakefield, is typical of what many 19th-century pits must have been like, with a cluster of rather small-scale buildings, from which rose wooden headgear and the chimney of a steam engine. Also near Wakefield was Silkstone Row, Altofts, an unusually long example of the type of terrace housing provided by a colliery owner, dating from *c.* 1860.

In the late 18th and 19th centuries, there was a great increase in demand for coal, due to the greater use being made of steam power, and also to the cheaper availability of mass-produced cast-iron fire grates and kitchen ranges. Steam engines and fireplaces were both made of cast iron, as indeed were the columns and beams used for many industrial buildings of the time. Low Mill Furnace, an 18th-century blast furnace, originally fitted with water-powered bellows, and still with its casting house complete, survives in a rural setting at Silkstone, near Barnsley. In Rosedale, high on the North York Moors, are mid-19th-century calcining kilns, used to reduce the weight of the ironstone mined nearby. The ore was transported in wagons along a steam-powered rope-hauled tramway, which climbed over 350m. to the level of a branch railway, where the kilns were situated.

Mining has traditionally been mainly associated with industrial west and south Yorkshire, although coal-mining is now moving north-eastwards with the development of the Selby coalfield. However, the Yorkshire Dales, nowadays commonly regarded as idyllic remote rural landscapes, once saw considerable industrial development, particularly associated with lead mining. The ore was refined fairly near its source, to reduce as far as possible the transportation problems of such a heavy material. A few of the smelting mills survive in which there were large furnaces, served by vast bellows, the operation of which was usually water powered. Near the village of Marrick in Swaledale there are the ruins of two mills, each with two large arches formerly over the hearths, the upper mill built *c.* 1860 around the 18th-century chimney of the lower mill. Near Grinton, there is another smelting mill, built *c.* 1820, the flue from which, now partly collapsed, climbed up from a mill a considerable distance on to the top of the moor before discharging its obnoxious fumes, first passing behind the nearby peat store, used to keep dry the fuel gathered annually on the surrounding moors.

The mines, as well as the smelting mills, were dangerous places to work. In the 18th and 19th centuries, black powder was used for blasting, and because it was so

239. Caphouse Colliery, Overton near Wakefield (MG).

volatile, it had to be stored in an isolated building. In Arkengarthdale there stands in a meadow a tiny, but beautifully-detailed powder magazine of *c.* 1804, which served the nearby 'C.B.' mines, named after the founder, Charles Bathurst. Close by is the C.B. Yard, a collection of houses formerly associated with the mines, and a little further away the *C.B. Inn.*

Another industry generally found in rural locations is that of limestone, quarried for building stone and also for calcinating to form a constituent of mortar, to be used for decorating purposes, and again as a dressing for the land, particularly in peaty soils. Near Kepwick, close to Northallerton, are the remains of lime-kilns, built into a hollow in the hillside, which served a quarry about three miles away, communication between the two being by means of a self-acting incline wagonway, which ran to the top of the kilns. On the outskirts of Northallerton are six lime-kilns, each of three furnaces, dated 1856, situated beside the Wensleydale railway line, along which the powdered lime could be despatched.

159

240. Silkstone Row, Altofts near Wakefield (MG).

241. Low Mill Furnace, Silkstone, near Barnsley (MG).

242. Low Mill Furnace, Silkstone, near Barnsley (MG).

243. Priest Royd Iron Works, Huddersfield, 1835: self-advertisement.

244. Upper Smelting Mill, Marrick in Swaledale, built around the chimney of the Lower Mill.

245. Arches to the furnaces, Marrick Upper Mill.

246. Grinton Smelting Mill, Swaledale, with the flue climbing up past the peat store and onto the top of the moor.

247. Peat Store, Grinton Smelting Mill.

248. Powder Magazine, Arkengarthdale.

249. Powder Magazine, with the C.B. Yard behind.

250. Details of kneelers, Powder Magazine.

Chalk from the Yorkshire Wolds was crushed to be used extensively as a whitening agent in paint, cosmetics, and even in food. A manufactory of chalk at Middleton-on-the-Wolds is of brick, with *in situ* concrete buttresses and louvred openings.

In areas without suitable supplies of building stone, clay was baked to form bricks and pantiles for building. After the coming of the railways, bricks from the London area and roofing slates from Wales were ubiquitously distributed throughout the country. Before that, small kilns provided bricks and pantiles for local consumption, which gave a characteristic appearance to local buildings, constructed with products of a size, colour and texture peculiar to that area. At the aptly-named Brickyard Farm at Slingsby, near Malton, is a derelict brick-kiln of chalk and brick.

Closely allied to the manufacture of brick is that of pottery, which was also once an everyday local industry. In the 18th century a few more industrialised establishments grew up, for instance, the Rockingham Pottery and the Leeds Pottery. The latter used a windmill to grind the flints used in the manufacture of its wares. In 1774, at the height of the success of the Leeds Pottery, a storm blew down the windmill. An alternative mill was hastily sought, and found near Wetherby, where a corn mill on the river Wharfe has just been rebuilt and was being advertised to let. The pottery rented the mill, and used it until the 19th century, finding it cheaper to import flints by sea, Ouse and Wharfe, as far as Flintmill, as the site became known, rather than taking them further inland along the Aire and Calder Navigation. A painting in York Minster Library shows the building at the time of its use as a flintmill. Later, it was converted back to being a corn mill.

251. Chalk Manufactory, Middleton-on-the-Wolds.

252. Brick kiln, Slingsby near Malton.

253. Brick kiln, Slingsby near Malton.

254. Flintmill near Wetherby (*York Minster Library*).

VII

MISCELLANEOUS INDUSTRIES

Some of the industries which do not fall within any of the other categories in this book are, or were, found in most areas—such as tanning; others are very specialised, and only a few can be included here. Until the early 20th century, most market towns had a tanyard; indeed, leather was so universally used in both towns and villages that a high proportion of craftsmen were involved in its preparation and application.

The preparation of leather seems to us nowadays a somewhat anti-social operation, for the processes are rather smelly, though no doubt our medieval ancestors were more reconciled to such matter than we are. Indeed, the traditional design of tanneries involved the provision of openings, not for the admittance of light, but for the emission of odour! Tanneries were also situated near streams, the water from which was used to fill and flush the curing pits. Small-scale tannery buildings usually consisted of small two- or three-storey buildings, with wooden louvred openings, in which skins were hung to be treated and dried. Such a building can be seen at Bridge Street, Helmsley, where the traditional site of the local tannery, beside the river Rye, is appropriately behind a butcher's shop, the two trades obviously being closely connected. In 1754, when there was a great flood down the Rye, which destroyed most of the bridges, the tan-pits and their contents were washed away, causing the tanner grave losses. In the 19th century, the tannery belonged to the Baxter family, who also had another tanyard at Lowna in Farndale.

Thomas Baxter, who bought the site at Lowna in 1801, was a man involved with many rural industries. Besides being a skinner, he dealt in wool, ground corn, and also crushed bones bought, like the hides, from butchers, for fertiliser. Because he had such a diverse operation, he could use the waterwheel of the corn mill to power the bone-crushing, and also a roller for reducing the oak bark, used in tanning processes, into nut-sized pieces. The last waterwheel, installed in 1887, also worked threshing machinery, a wood saw, and a pump which circulated water through the tan-pits.

In the country, there was no incentive to rebuild the tannery on a monumental scale; in Leeds, where there were many tanneries in the 19th century, the almost contemporary Oak Tannery at Kirkstall, of 1876, had an imposing facade, with the name and date carved in stone, adorned by a sculpture of a bullock's head as the centrepiece.

Paper-making is an industry which, in a small way, typifies the Industrial Revolution and post-industrialisation. It was not until the 19th century that quality paper became more cheaply available. During the 18th century there was a sharp increase in the number of small paper mills, which mainly manufactured from rags a coarse, brown paper used increasingly for wrapping. A few mills made paper for newspaper, or book printing, then a growth area due to an upsurge in literacy. In the 19th century, techno-

255. Tannery in Bridge Street, Helmsley.

256. Oak Tannery, Kirkstall, Leeds, of 1876 (MG).

logical developments revolutionised the paper-making process, which resulted in fewer, but larger paper mills, and the closure of the small ones. In the 20th century, that trend has continued, and now very few large, modern paper mills serve the country's needs.

One of only about 40 paper mills recorded in the country in the early 17th century was at Old Byland, near Helmsley. By the late 17th century there were two others, both at Thornton Dale, near Pickering, in the North Riding, and about nine in the West Riding, including one at Sheepscar, near Leeds, another at Thorp Arch, and a third beside the North Bridge in Halifax. A picture of an 18th-century Yorkshire paper mill is in the collection of York Minster Library. It shows a group of ramshackle buildings besides the river Swale at St Martins, near Richmond. The buildings are in stone, with thatched roofs, and have louvred openings not, like tanneries, to let out a foul smell, but to dry the sheets of paper laboriously produced by hand one at a time on a small frame. St Martins Mill was operated by one James Cooke, whose kinsman, Henry Cooke, built a much larger paper mill near Richmond *c.* 1825, using a machine, developed by Fourdrinier, for producing larger quantities of paper.

257. St Martins Paper Mill near Richmond in the 18th century
(*York Minster Library*).

258. Alf Cooke and Sons Ltd., Leeds (MG).

259. Airedale Works, Leeds (MG).

260. Yorkshire Evening Press Office, Coney Street, York.

Closely related to paper mills are printing works, several of which have fine buildings. Printers, like cloth merchants, have need of a close relationship with the general public, more than factory owners, hence the desire for polite architecture. In Leeds, Alf Cooke and Sons, in a position given more prominence by its proximity to motorway access roads, is another Leeds building influenced by the Moorish style of architecture, and the Airedale Works has fine terracotta Art Nouveau decoration. In York, the *Yorkshire Evening Press* office, besides the river Ouse, has neo-classical details picked out in polychromatic brickwork.

York, not generally thought of as an industrial city, has several large sweet and chocolate manufacturers. The oldest chocolate factory building in the city is Rowntree's old factory of the 1880s in Tanners Moat, with a water tank for an early sprinkler system above the roof near the steam-engine chimney. It was replaced only a few years later by a much larger factory on the Haxby Road, and the Quaker family owners also turned their attention to the philanthropic idea of New Earswick model village. This attitude contrasts with that of Mackintosh's in Halifax, with whom the company is now amalgamated, which built in the early 20th century a rather imposing factory.

171

261. Rowntree's old factory, Tanners Moat, York.

262. Mackintosh's factory, Halifax (MG).

263. Smoke house chimneys, Ropery Street, off Hessle Road, Hull.

264. Entrance to Chicory Yard, Layerthorpe, York.

Cocoa beans were imported into England and, although they were brought by river transport to York, it seems that the reasons for York having such an important chocolate industry are largely due to chance factors, such as the interests, enterprise and business acumen of individual families. There was a more obvious reason for the location in Hull of an industry which produced a very distinctive architectural form. Smoke houses, for the curing of fish, were small buildings with steeply-pitched roofs surmounted by tall cowls. Most have now disappeared.

York once had a much more unusual industry than that of chocolate-making: chicory roasting. Chicory, a root crop similar to the parsnip, was extensively grown in the Dunnington area to the east of York. Introduced *c.* 1840, its cultivation required careful tending, which provided casual work for large numbers of poor people. The root was dried and roasted, and ground up for use as a beverage, a use which attracted tax in 1860. In 1863 the tax on home-grown, but not on imported, chicory was increased, an anomaly which effectively destroyed the Dunnington industry. The roasting kilns there were abandoned, and the declining trade became centred on York, where the leading merchant was Thomas 'Chicory' Smith, whose works were in Layerthorpe, the aroma from which frequently wafted over the city. Now only the sign above an alley opening there—Chicory Yard—serves as a reminder of an important, if short-lived, phenomenon of industrial history and architecture.

INDEX

(Plate numbers in *italics*)